Hama on the Rebel River

حماة على النهر العاصي

Stephen Lumsden, Georges Mouamar,
Anne Haslund Hansen & Mette Marie Hald

Hama on the Rebel River

A Syrian Town in the 1930s through the Eyes of Danish Archaeologists

ستيفن لومسدن، جورج معمر، آن هاسلوند هانسن، ميت ماري هالد

حماة على النهر العاصي

مدينةٌ سوريةٌ بعيون علماء الآثار الدنماركيين في ثلاثينيات القرن الماضي

PROCEEDINGS OF THE DANISH INSTITUTE IN DAMASCUS 18
AARHUS UNIVERSITY PRESS

Hama on the Rebel River
Proceedings of the Danish Institute in Damascus, 18

Cover, layout and typesetting: Carl-H.K. Zakrisson
Cover illustration: Ḥāmid al-Kīlānī
Publishing editor: Sanne Lind Hansen
This book is typeset in Brill og Arial and printed on 150 g Arctic Matt
Printed by Specialtrykkeriet Arco, Denmark

Printed in Denmark 2023

ISBN 978 87 7597 143 5

Aarhus University Press
aarhusuniversitypress.dk

Published with the financial support of
the Danish Institute in Damascus and the National Museum of Denmark

International distributors

Oxbow Books Ltd., oxbowbooks.com
ISD, isdistribution.com

FSC www.fsc.org MIX Papir fra ansvarlige kilder FSC® C010493

SVANEMÆRKET Tryksag 5041 0826

Acknowledgements

The idea for this book came about while three of the book's authors worked on an archaeological research project about ancient Hama, generously supported by Independent Research Fund Denmark ("Ordinary Lives in Extraordinary Times: A New View of the Earliest Urban Societies in Bronze Age Syria" – grant number 1024–00107B, award holder: Mette Marie Hald).

While the research project has focused specifically on life in Early Bronze Age Hama, we were struck by the vast archive material pertaining to contemporary Hama during the Danish excavations in the 1930s. This book therefore came about as an independent project.

The authors are grateful to Mirella Mouamar and Moussa El-Khoury for advice on the Arabic translation, and to Inger Marie Helgasdatter Mulvad, Maximillian Holmström, and Lasse Sommer Schütt for help with image digitalization.

Publication of the book was made possible with generous financial support from the Danish Institute in Damascus and the National Museum of Denmark.

كلمة شكر

جاءت فكرة هذا الكتاب من خلال عمل ثلاثة من مؤلفيه على مشروع بحثٍ أثريٍ حول مدينة حماة القديمة، بدعمٍ من صندوق الأبحاث الدنماركي المستقل. ركز مشروع البحث بشكل خاص على الحياة في عصر البرونز القديم في مدينة حماة خلال الألف الثالث قبل الميلاد، خلال العمل على المشروع أدهشتنا المواد الأرشيفية الهائلة المتعلقة بالمدينة والمعاصرة للحفريات الدنماركية خلال ثلاثينيات القرن الماضي. لذلك جاء هذا الكتاب كمشروع مستقل.

يتوجه المؤلفون بالشكر والتقدير لكل من ميريلا معمر وموسى الخوري للحصول على المشورة بشأن الترجمة العربية، ولإنجر ماري هيلجاسداتر مولفاد وماكسيميليان هولمستروم ولاسي سومير شوت للمساعدة في رقمنة الصور.

تم نشر هذا الكتاب بدعم مالي من قبل المعهد الدنماركي بدمشق والمتحف الوطني الدنماركي.

Introduction

The large mound in the town of Hama is well known in Syrian archaeology for the excavations there by a Danish team in the 1930s. However, in addition to their archaeological investigations that were mainly undertaken on the mound, the Danes also documented the town around the mound at that time, and that is what this book is about. The photographs, architectural plans, and watercolours that make up this archive, many of which have not been previously published, are a priceless record of a place and a time that no longer exist.

Hama is located on the Orontes River in Inland Western Syria. In Arabic, the Orontes is called the Rebel ('Aāṣī) River, probably because among all the major rivers in the region it is the only one that flows south to north (rather than north to south). Hama is located on what has always been the most important north-south route in this part of the Middle East, what in Ottoman times was called the "Sultanic Road". This road extended from Anatolia in the north through Aleppo, Hama, Homs, and Damascus and then south through Palestine to the Hijaz and Egypt; it was the principal road for merchants, pilgrims, and soldiers. It is also the intersection of several productive landscapes at Hama that has contributed to the successful settlement history here: the river flood plain is suitable for gardens and orchards (the famous waterwheels at Hama have been employed at least since Late Roman times to lift water from the river); there is enough annual precipitation to support dry farming in the rich agricultural soil around the town – it is one of the most intensely farmed areas in Western Syria; and not far to the east, steppe land serves as summer pastures for Bedouin tribes.

The over 40-meter-high mound at Hama dominated the surrounding town in the 1930s. Hama is, in fact, the oldest continuously lived in town in Syria (from the mid-7th millennium BCE to the present – around 8500 years of continuous settlement). Highlights include its role as a holy city in the Early Bronze Age, Period IV (ca 2500–2000 BCE), an important pilgrimage destination. Hamath, as it was known in the Iron Age (ca 1000–600 BCE), was a powerful local kingdom that opposed the mighty Assyrians until its destruction at the hands of

Sargon II in 720 BCE. Under the Romans, a detachment of archers from Hama (*Cohors Prima Hamiorum Sagittaria*) served from 120 CE at Hadrian's Wall in Northern Britain. Hama was conquered by the Muslims in 638 and was subsequently ruled by the Umayyads, Abbasids, the Egyptian Fatimids, Turkish Seljuks, and the Crusaders. In 1175, Hama was taken by the most famous foe of the Crusaders, Saladin. After the Mongol Tamerlane (Timur Lenk) destroyed the town in 1400, the mound was never reoccupied. During the Ottoman Period, between the 14th century and the early 20th century, Hama expanded in size with the growth of regional trade. It became more closely linked to the new centre of regional wealth, power, and culture in Damascus and became an agricultural entrepôt that provided grain for the annual pilgrimage (Ḥaj) caravans.

In the 1930s, Hama was the fourth largest town in French Mandatory Syria, after Damascus, Aleppo, and nearby Homs. By 1930 the population had reached 60,000, mostly Sunni Muslims with a small Greek Orthodox Christian minority. Other minorities living in the Hama governate included Alawites, Circassians, Ismailis, Kurds, and Turkomans. In addition to the strong agricultural sector, Hama was an important producer of textiles and leather goods. The town was bisected by the Orontes River. On the west bank, west and southwest of the mound (al-Qal'a), lay the oldest part of the town, al-Madina, with its narrow winding alleyways. The Great Mosque was located here, as was the Christian neighbourhood and Greek Orthodox cathedral. The two main markets (sūqs) in the old part of town were located in the vicinity of the Great Mosque and near the Nūrī mosque, on the banks of the river. A labyrinth of streets connected this part of the town with that farther south of the mound, the al-Dabāġa quarter, in which was located an old caravansary that served as the Danish Expedition's quarters in the later years of the project, Khān Rustm Bāshā. On the east bank of the river lay the newer part of the town, al-Ḥāḍir. Here folk had settled permanently outside the walls of the old town. The al-Madina and al-Ḥāḍir quarters were joined by the bridge called Jisr Bayt al-Shaykh (The Bridge at the Shaykh's House). North of the mound was located the town cemetery, and to the northwest, the French military encampment. A number of waterwheels and connected aqueducts brought water from the river to particular buildings and to gardens and orchards around the town.

This was the town that the Danish team members visually documented over the course of the Expedition, from 1931 to 1938. It was one of the best-preserved Ottoman Period towns in the region and was characterized as one of the most picturesque and least westernized towns in Syria, with an almost medieval feel to it. The images in this book were in the main produced by members of the Danish Expedition. They had come to find the remains of an ancient town that had ceased to exist long ago, and along the way captured through letters, photographs, and watercolours another town that has since also faded into the past. The photos are snapshots of life in the town seen through the eyes of curious Europeans, who, on the one hand were in the field to carry out their research in archaeology, and on the other were on an adventure of a lifetime, entranced by the place around them. They took photos of Ottoman houses, waterwheels, celebrations, and people going about their daily lives. Some images are blurry, capturing moments of people on the move and sheep being herded through the narrow streets. The watercolours, on the other hand, present a more serene view of the town, most especially of the grand mansions of the urban elite, but also of town squares and alleyways.

The onset of a new archaeological project studying the artifacts from the excavations at Hama stored in the National Museum of Denmark has led to the publication of this book. The authors – from afar – are again studying the ancient societies revealed by the excavations on the mound in the 1930s and are again both entranced by the surrounding town and curious about its inhabitants, as revealed in the photographs and watercolours in the archive. In our version of the story of Hama in the 1930s, however, we accompany the Danish images that portray a peaceful and picturesque representation of an old-fashioned way of life with texts that relate the political and social turmoil beneath the apparently tranquil surface that also characterized Hama in French Mandatory Syria in the 1930s.

مقدمة

إن التل الأثري الكبير الواقع في قلب مدينة حماة معروف جيداً في علم الآثار السورية بفضل الحفريات والأبحاث التي قام بها فريقٌ دنماركي في ثلاثينيات القرن الماضي في الموقع. وعلاوةً على أبحاثهم الآثارية التي تركَّزت بشكلٍ أساسي على التل، وثَّق الدنماركيون مدينة حماة الممتدة حول التل الأثري في ذلك الوقت، وهذا تحديداً ما يتمحور حوله موضوع هذا الكتاب. وفي الواقع يحتفظ المتحف الوطني الدنماركي بأرشيف نادر لمكانٍ وزمانٍ لم يعد لهما وجود، ويتألف هذا الأرشيف من مجموعة كبيرة من الصور والمخططات المعمارية واللوحات بالألوان المائية لم يُنشر الكثير منها سابقاً.

تقعُ مدينة حماة على نهر العاصي في المنطقة الداخلية لسوريا الوسطى الغربية. يُطلق على نهر العاصي في اللغة العربية هذا الاسم (أي العاصي)، لأنَّه النهر الوحيد من بين جميع الأنهار الرئيسيَّة في منطقة بلاد الشام الذي يتدفَّقُ من الجنوب إلى الشمال (بدلاً من الشمال إلى الجنوب). تقعُ حماة على أحد أهم الطرق في هذا الجزء من الشرق الأوسط، وهو ما كان يطلقُ عليه في العهد العثماني «الطريق السلطاني». امتد هذا الطريق من الأناضول شمالاً مروراً بحلب وحماة وحمص ودمشق، ثمَّ جنوباً عبر فلسطين إلى الحجاز ومصر، وكان الطريق الرئيسيُّ للتجَّار والحجاج والجنود. تتقاطع أيضاً في حماة العديد من البيئات الإنتاجية مما ساهم في نجاح تاريخ الاستيطان فيها. فالسهلُ الفيضي للنهر ملائمٌ جداً للحدائق والبساتين (تمَّ استخدام النواعير الشهيرة في حماة لرفع المياه من النهر منذ العصر الروماني المتأخر على أقل تقدير)؛ وهناك ما يكفي من معدل الأمطار السنويَّة لدعم الزراعة الجافة في التربة الزراعية الغنية حول المدينة، وهي واحدةٌ من أكثر المناطق المزروعة بكثافة غربي سوريا؛ وليس بعيدًا إلى الشرق، كانت تُستخدم الأراضي على تخوم البادية السورية كمراعٍ صيفيَّة للقبائل البدويَّة.

هيمنت تلَّة حماة الأثريَّة التي يزيد ارتفاعها عن أربعين متراً على محيط المدينة في ثلاثينيات القرن الماضي. تُعتبر مدينة حماة أقدم مدينةٍ مأهولةٍ في سوريا (لم تنقطع فيها الحياة منذ منتصف الألفيَّة السابعة قبل الميلاد حتى الوقت الحاضر «أي ما يقارب ٨٥٠٠ عام من الاستيطان المستمر»). من أبرز المفاصل التاريخيَّة لمدينة حماة، دورها كمدينةٍ مقدسةٍ خلال عصر البرونز القديم الرابع (حوالي ٢٠٠٠-٢٥٠٠ قبل الميلاد) حيث كانت مقصداً مهماً للحجّ في تلك الفترة بحسب ما ورد في وثائق مملكة إبلا. توسّعت حماة وازدهرت في العهد الآرامي (العصر الحديدي، حوالي ٦٠٠-١٠٠٠ قبل الميلاد)، وتشكّلت فيها مملكةٌ محليةٌ قويةٌ عارضت الآشوريين الأقوياء حتى دمارها على يد سرجون الثاني في العام ٧٢٠ قبل الميلاد. تحت حكم الرومان وتحديداً عام ١٢٠م، خدمت مفرزة من رماة السهام من مدينة حماة (*Cohors Prima Hamiorum Sagittaria*) على جدار هادريان شمالي بريطانيا. فتح المسلمون حماة عام ٦٣٨م وحكمها الأمويون والعباسيون والفاطميون المصريون والسلاجقة الأتراك والصليبيون. في العام ١١٧٥م استولى صلاح الدين أشهرُ أعداءِ الصليبيين على حماة. بعد دمار المدينة في العام ١٤٠٠م على يد المغول (تيمورلنك) هُجر التلُّ القديم ولم تعد له الحياة أبدًا. خلال الفترة العثمانيَّة، بين القرن الرابع عشر وأوائل القرن العشرين، أصبحت حماة مدينةً هامةً، وتوسّعت في الحجم مع نمو التجارة الإقليميَّة. وغدت أكثر ارتباطاً بالمركز الجديد للثروة والسلطة والثقافة في دمشق، كما باتت مخزناً زراعياً يوفِّر الحبوب لقوافل الحج السنويَّة.

في ثلاثينيات القرن الماضي، كانت حماة رابع أكبر مدينةٍ في سوريا خلال فترة الانتداب الفرنسي، بعد دمشق وحلب وحمص المجاورة لها، وبحلول العام ١٩٣٠، وصل عدد السكان فيها إلى ٦٠٠٠٠ نسمة، معظمهم من المسلمين السُنَّة مع أقليةٍ مسيحيةٍ أرثوذكسية. من بين الأقليات الأخرى التي تعيش في محافظة حماة العلويون والإسماعيليون والتركمان والشركس والأكراد.

يَفصُل العاصي حماة إلى شطرين. على الضفة الغربية، ويقع غربي وجنوبي غرب التل أقدم جزءٍ من المدينة (حماة القديمة) مع أزقتها الضيقة المتعرّجة. في هذا الجزء من المدينة يتواجد الجامع الكبير وكذلك الحي المسيحي وكاتدرائية الروم الأرثوذكس. كان السوقان الرئيسيان في الجزء القديم من المدينة يقعان في محيط الجامع الكبير وبالقرب من مسجد النوري على ضفاف النهر. ربطت متاهةٌ من الشوارع هذا الجزء من المدينة مع أقصى التل من جهة الجنوب، حي الدباغة،

الذي كان يقع فيه« خان رُستم باشا» القديم والذي كان بمثابة مقرٍّ للبعثة الدنماركية في السنوات الأخيرة من المشروع. على الضفة الشرقية للنهر يقع الجزء الأحدث من المدينة،« حي الحاضر»، هنا بدأ السكّان الاستقرار بشكل دائم خارج أسوار المدينة القديمة. كان يربط حي الحاضر بالمدينة القديمة جسر يسمى جسر بيت الشيخ. في الجهة الشمالية من التل كانت تقع مقبرة المدينة، وفي الشمال الغربي كانت معسكرات الجيش الفرنسيّ. في تلك الفترة، لعبت النواعير دوراً أساسياً في اقتصاد مدينة حماة، إذ كان يتم رفع ماء النهر عن طريق عدد كبير من النواعير المنتشرة على جانبي النهر، ومن ثم يُنقل عبر قنوات محمولة على قناطر لتُسقى به البساتين والحمامات وبعض الدور والجوامع والخانات والمقاهي.

كانت هذه هي المدينة التي وثَّقها أعضاءُ الفريق الدنماركي بصرياً خلال رحلتهم الاستكشافية التي امتدت من العام ١٩٣١ إلى العام ١٩٣٨. كانت حماة واحدة من أفضلِ مدن الفترة العثمانيَّة التي تم الحفاظ عليها في المنطقة، وتميّزت بأنها واحدةٌ من أكثر المدن جمالاً وروعةً، والأقلُّ تأثّراً بالغرب حيث يطغى عليها طابع القرون الوسطى.

معظم الأشكال والصور الموجودة في هذا الكتاب تم توثيقها وتنفيذها بواسطة أعضاء البعثة الدنماركية، الذين اختاروا تل حماة الأثري بحثاً عن بقايا مدينةٍ قديمةٍ لم تعد موجودة منذ زمن بعيدٍ، وخلال رحلة بحثهم وثَّقوا بالحرف والصور الفوتوغرافية والألوان المائية مدينةً أخرى أَحدث تلاشت أيضاً منذُ ذلك الحين في الماضي.

الصور هي للقطاتٍ من الحياة اليومية في المدينة وثقتها عيون الأوروبيين الفضوليين، الذين كانوا من ناحيةٍ في الميدان لإجراء أبحاثهم في علم الآثار، وكانوا من ناحيةٍ أخرى في مغامرة العمر، مفتونين بجمال وروعة المكان المحيط بهم. لقد التقطوا صوراً للمنازل من الفترة العثمانية واحتفالات المدينة والنواعير المائية والسكان المحليين الذين يمارسون حياتهم اليوميَّة. من جهة أخرى، تقدّم لوحات الألوان المائية منظراً أكثر هدوء للمدينة، لا سيما القصور الكبرى للنخبة الحضرية، ولكن أيضاً لساحات المدينة ولأزقتها.

هذا الكتاب هو أحَّد ثمار مشروع الدراسة الآثارية الجديد الذي يهدف إلى دراسة القطع الأثرية التي عُثر عليها من قبل البعثة الدنماركية في حماة والمحفوظة في المتحف الوطني الدنماركي. يدرس المؤلفون من خلال هذا المشروع المجتمعات القديمة التي كشفت عنها الحفريات على التل الأثري في ثلاثينيات القرن الماضي، وهم أيضاً كما من سبقهم مفتونون جداً بالمدينة القديمة المحيطة بالتل وينتابهم الفضول بشأن سكانها، كما تظهرهم الصور ولوحات الألوان المائية في الأرشيف.

في نسختنا من قصة حماة في ثلاثينيات القرن الماضي، نرافق الصور الدنماركية التي ترسم صورة سلمية وخلابة لطريقة عيش قديمة مع نصوص تروي الاضطرابات السياسية والاجتماعية المتخفية تحت هذا السطح الهادئ الظاهر والتي ميَّزت مدينة حماة خلال فترة الانتداب الفرنسي على سوريا في الثلاثينيات من القرن الماضي.

Regional states of Syria during the French Mandate 1920–1946
Map: Georges Mouamar (after Don-kun, Wikimedia Commons)

The Arabic-speaking regions in the Middle East were part of the Ottoman Empire for 400 years. After the Ottoman defeat in the First World War, the part of the empire that became Syria and Lebanon was ruled by France as a colony from 1920 to 1946, known as the French Mandate.

خارطة الانتداب الفرنسي على سوريا عام ١٩٢٠ـ١٩٤٦
الخريطة: جورج معمر

كانت المناطق الناطقة باللغة العربية في الشرق الأوسط جزءً من الإمبراطورية العثمانية لمدة أربعمائة عام. في أعقاب هزيمة العثمانيين في الحرب العالميَّة الأولى، وَقَعَ جزءٌ من هذه الإمبراطورية تحت الانتداب الفرنسي بين الأعوام ١٩٢٠ إلى ١٩٤٦م. بعد انتهاء فترة الانتداب في أواخر أربعينيات القرن العشرين نشأ كيانان مستقلان هما الجمهورية السورية والجمهورية اللبنانية.

The building on the left of the photo is the first Expedition house (1931-35), Baīt Sa'īd Bak Fardūs Al-'Aẓm. Photo: Mathilius Elo, 1931.

المبنى الموجود على يسار الصورة هو أول بيت للبعثة الدنماركية في حماة (١٩٣١-١٩٣٥)، بيت سعيد بك فردوس العظم. الصورة: ماتيليوس إيلو، عام ١٩٣١

Hama mound and the surrounding town
Photo: Hama Expedition, 1936

Aerial view towards the south, of the mound and town, with the Orontes River and the Shaykh Bridge on the left. The main areas of excavation during the Danish Expedition are visible in the photo – the deep trench in the centre of the mound that reached the Late Neolithic Period and the excavations at the southern end of the mound that revealed the Iron Age citadel. Like other Western excavations in the Middle East during this period, the Danes concentrated on the pre-Islamic periods on the mound. Although the Danish archaeologists did not represent an imperial power in this part of the world, Western archaeology in the Middle East in general, from the 19th century through the 1930s, played a role in the colonial projects of Great Britain and France. As the "handmaid of imperialism" in this period, archaeology served the political goals of the imperial powers by disengaging the local populace from their deep past, creating a narrative that both traced a direct lineage of the cultures of the pre-Islamic Middle East to the West, and, in bypassing the current inhabitants, constructed the "non-West".

تلُّ حماة الأثري والمدينة المجاورة
الصورة: البعثة الدنماركية في حماة، عام ١٩٣٦

صورةٌ جويَّةٌ مأخوذةٌ باتجاه الجنوب للتلِّ الأثري ومدينة حماة. يظهر فيها على الجهة اليسرى نهر العاصي وجسر بيت الشيخ، كما تظهر بشكلٍ واضحٍ أماكن التنقيب والحفريات الأثريَّة التي قامت بها البعثة الدنماركية على التلِّ الأثري. في وسط التلِّ نشاهد السبر الأثري العميق الذي مكَّننا من الوصول إلى الاستيطان الأقدم لمدينة حماة والعائد إلى العصر الحجري الحديث المتأخِّر، كما تظهر أيضاً الحفريات المنفَّذة في أقصى الجهة الجنوبية والتي كشفت عن قلعةِ العصرِ الآرامي.

تركَّزت الحفريات الدنماركية، كما معظم الحفريات الغربيَّة الأخرى في الشرق الأوسط، خلال هذه الفترة على عصور ما قبل الإسلام. وهنا تجدرُ الإشارة إلى أنَّ علماء الآثار الدنماركيين لم يمثِّلوا أيَّ قوةٍ سياسيةٍ عالميةٍ في ذلك الوقت، على عكس الكثير من المشاريع الأثريَّة الغربيَّة في الشرق الأوسط، التي عملت من القرن التاسع عشر وحتى ثلاثينيات القرن الماضي، والتي لعبت دوراً في المشاريع الاستعمارية لإنجلترا وفرنسا. خدم علم الآثار في هذه الفترة، الأهداف السياسية للقوى الإمبريالية من خلال فكِّ ارتباط السكَّان المحليين عن ماضيهم العميق، وذلك عن طريق خلق رواياتٍ وسردياتٍ تَنسِبُ ثقافات الشرق الأوسط ما قبل الإسلام إلى الغرب.

A glimpse of an 8500-year-long history
Drawing, Dan Shadrake, 2020; photos: Hama Expedition (lion), Georges Mouamar (ploughshare), Kit Weiss (Islamic bowl).

Lion statue from the Iron Age (ca. 1000–600 BCE) citadel, previously exhibited in the National Museum of Denmark; Hamian Archer from the Roman cohort guarding Hadrian's Wall in northern Britain ca. 120 CE; Basalt ploughshare, Early Bronze Age; Islamic Period bowl, Syrian production, first half of the 13th century.

لمحةٌ عن تاريخٍ يمتدُّ لـ ٨٥٠٠ عام
الرسم: دان شادريك،٢٠٢٠؛ الصور: البعثة الدنماركية في حماة (الأسد)، جورج معمر (المحراث)، كيت فايس (صحن الفخار الإسلامي)

تمثالٌ لأسدٍ من حجر البازلت، عُثر عليه في قلعة العصر الآرامي (حوالي ١٠٠٠ ـ ٦٠٠ قبل الميلاد) وعُرض سابقاً في المتحف الوطني الدنماركي؛ صورة لرامي سهامٍ من حماة والتابع للفوج العسكري الروماني الذي شارك في حراسة جدار هادريان في شمال بريطانيا عام ١٢٠م؛ رأس محراث من حجر البازلت يعود لعصر البرونز القديم؛ صورة لآنيةٍ من الفخار وهي من إنتاجٍ سوري تعود للفترة الإسلامية، وتحديداً للنصف الأول من القرن الثالث عشر الميلادي.

D. Snadrake. 20

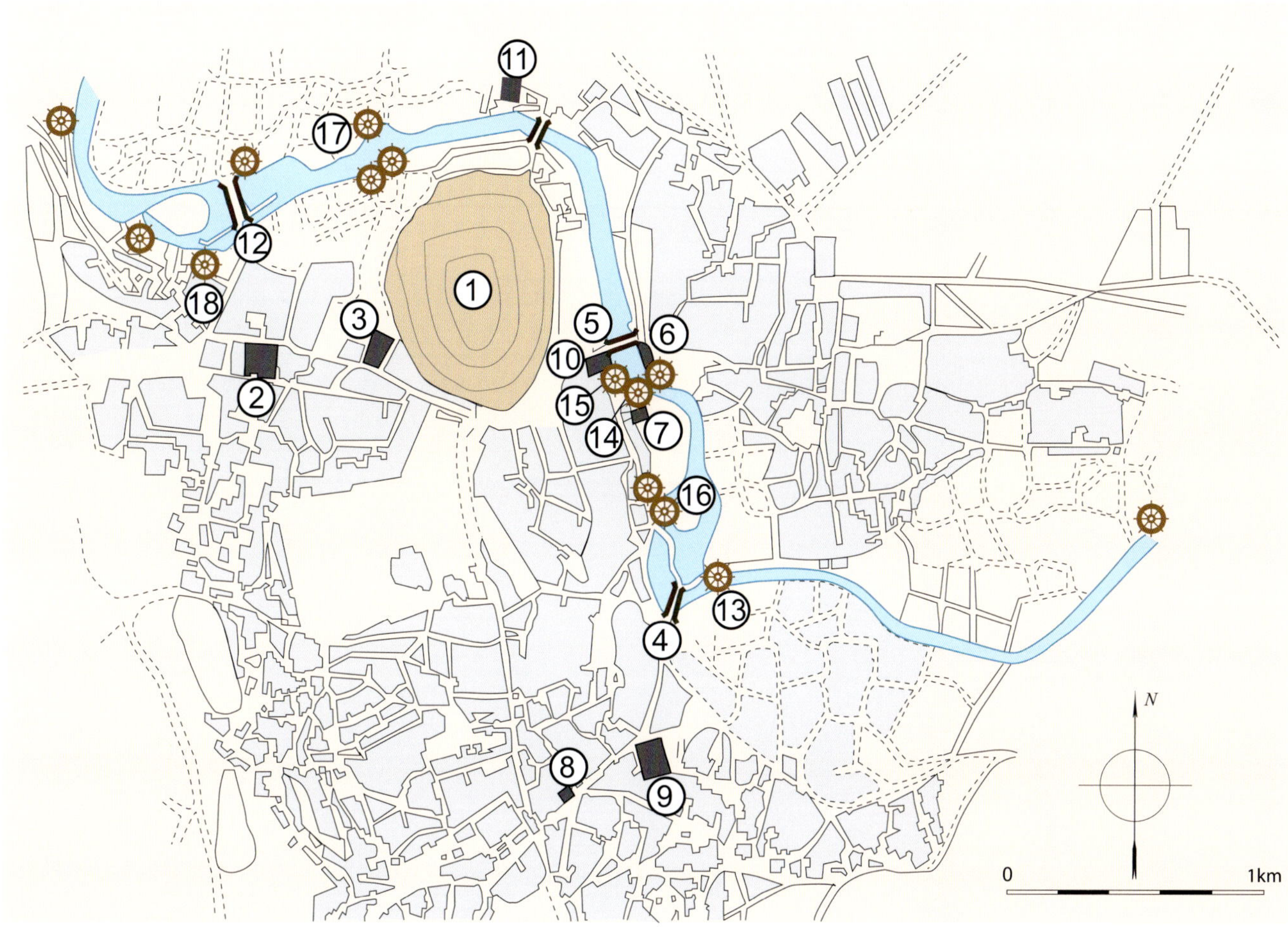

Plan of 1930s Hama

Plan: Georges Mouamar, after Nilsson 2002:18.

Location of the mound, the waterwheels, and buildings mentioned in the text.

1. Tell Hama (the Citadel)
2. Great Mosque
3. Greek Orthodox cathedral
4. Al-Sarāyā Bridge
5. Bayt Al-Shaykh Bridge (Al-Kīlāniya)
6. Al-Kīlānī Mansion
7. Al-ʻAẓm Palace
8. Ḥammām Darwīsh Bāshā (Al-Darwīshiya)
9. Khān Rustm Bāshā
10. Al-Nūrī Mosque
11. ʼAbī Al-Fidāʼ Mosque
12. Bāb al-Nahir Bridge
13. Waterwheel – Al- Jisriyah
14. Waterwheel – Al- Ṣahyūniyah
15. Waterwheel – Al-Juʻbariyah
16. Waterwheel – Al-Ma'mūriyah
17. Waterwheel – Al-Dahshah
18. Waterwheel – Al-Muḥamadyah

خارطة مدينة حماة في ثلاثينيات القرن الماضي

الخارطة: جورج معمر

توضّحُ الخارطة موقع التلّ الأثري وأماكن توزُّع النواعير بالإضافة إلى المباني المذكورة في هذا الكتاب.

١. تل حماة (القلعة)
٢. الجامع الكبير
٣. كاتدرائية الروم الأرثوذكس
٤. جسر السرايا
٥. جسر بيت الشيخ «جسر الكيلانية»
٦. قصر الكيلاني
٧. قصر العظم
٨. حمَّام درويش باشا «الدرويشيَّة»
٩. خان رستم باشا
١٠. جامع النوري
١١. جامع وضريح أبي الفداء
١٢. جسر باب النهر
١٣. ناعورة الجسرية
١٤. ناعورة الصهيونية
١٥. ناعورة الجعبرية
١٦. ناعورة المأموريَّة
١٧. ناعورة الدهشة
١٨. ناعورة المحمديَّة

The Hama mound with the surrounding town and Orontes River
Photo: Hama Expedition, 1936

Aerial view of the mound and immediately surrounding urban terrain. Visible are the Orontes River flowing alongside the eastern flank of the mound and parts of the old town (al-Madina) on the left of the photo and the more recent housing – but still quite old – east of the river on the right of the photo (al-Ḥāḍir). The Shaykh Bridge across the river that joined the two parts of the town at the Nūrī Mosque and Kīlānī Mansion is also visible. Some of the gardens watered by means of the waterwheels (*nā'ūra*) can be seen to the left of the mound and above the al-Madina quarter. The different character of the two quarters is apparent – the tightly packed houses along narrow, winding alleyways of al-Madina in contrast to the more open aspect of al-Ḥāḍir. The walled compound of the Greek Orthodox cathedral, including a cemetery, can be seen in the old town adjacent to the gardens. The Christian quarter was located in the old town, although Christians and Muslims also lived together in other neighbourhoods.

تلُّ حماة والمدينة المحيطة به مع نهر العاصي
الصورة: البعثة الدنماركية في حماة، عام ١٩٣٦

صورةٌ جويةٌ لتلِّ حماة مع النسيج العمراني المحيط به، يَختِرقُ المشهد نهر العاصي وهو يتدفَّق على طول الجانب الشرقي من التلِّ. على يسار الصورة تظهر أجزاءٌ من المدينة القديمة، في الجزء العلوي على يمين الصورة وشرقي النهر نرى حي الحاضر، وهو القسم الأحدث من المدينة. كما يظهر جلياً جسر بيت الشيخ (جسر الكيلانية) الذي يربط شطري المدينة عند مسجد النوري وقصر الكيلاني. يمكن أيضاً رؤية بعض الحدائق التي تُسقى بواسطة النواعير والمتمركزة بشكل رئيسي على الجهة اليسرى للتلِّ. من خلال هذه الصورة يتضح الطابع المختلف للحيَّين، ففي المدينة القديمة تنتشر المنازل المكتظَّة بإحكامٍ على طول الأزقَّة الضيِّقة والمتعرِّجة على عكس الطابع الأكثر انفتاحاً المميَّز لحي الحاضر. في المدينة القديمة وتحديداً في القسم المجاور للتلِّ والحدائق يمكن رؤية المجمَّع المسوَّر لكاتدرائية الروم الأرثوذكس وكذلك المقبرة. كان الحي المسيحيُّ يقع في المدينة القديمة، على الرغم من أنَّ المسيحيين والمسلمين كانوا يعيشون معاً في أحياءٍ أخرى.

View from the mound towards the southwest at al-Madina neighbourhood
Photo: Hama Expedition, 1938

Part of the Greek Orthodox cathedral compound is in the foreground to the right. In the middle foreground can be seen typically Ottoman-style houses with the characteristic overhanging upper storey (Arabic *mashrabīah*), which allowed for shade as well as undisturbed views of street life for the women of the house. On top of the hill in the centre in the distance is the French Commandant's house in the neighbourhood Bāb al-Qiblī, where the Great Mosque was located.

منظرٌ من تلِّ حماة باتجاه الجنوب الغربي والمدينة القديمة
الصورة: البعثة الدنماركية في حماة، عام ١٩٣٨

في مقدِّمة الصورة من الجهة اليمنى يَظهرُ جزءٌ من مجمَّع كاتدرائية الروم الأرثوذكس. على قمَّة الهضبة في الوسط، يقعُ منزل القائد الفرنسي في حي باب القبلي حيث كان المسجد الكبير. بجوار الكاتدرائية يمكن رؤية المنازل ذات الطراز العثماني النموذجي والمتميزة بعنصر معماري يطلق عليه «المشربية» وهو عنصر معماري يتمثَّل في بروز الغرف في الطابق الأول أو ما فوقه بحيث يمتدُّ فوق الشارع، يكثر استخدام المشربيات في القصور والبيوت التقليديَّة (المباني السكنيّة)، إلا أنها استُخدمت أيضاً في بعض المباني العامة. هذا الطراز المعماري ملائمٌ لتوفير الظِّل كما يسمحُ للنساء باختلاس النظر على حياة الشارع بأمانٍ

View from the French Commandant's house in Bāb al-Qiblī towards the southeast, with a sports field in the centre
Photo: Hama Expedition, 1938

The colonial overlords have often been seen as agents of change in the Middle East in the first half of the 20th century, implying that modernization was a gift from the European powers. However, already in the Ottoman Period in the late 19th and early 20th centuries mass education had been established and new forms of public life, like sports and other recreational activities, had become popular. These trends continued into the 1930s. In 1937 at Hama, students petitioned for either the reopening of an athletic club that had been closed in 1933 by the French authorities or the appointment of a physical education teacher at their school, based on the sentiment that the new Syria required physically fit youth.

منظرٌ من منزل القائد الفرنسي في باب القبلي باتجاه الجنوب الشرقي، مع ملعبٍ رياضيٍ في الوسط
الصورة: البعثة الدنماركية في حماة، عام ١٩٣٨

غالباً ما كان يُنظر في النصف الأوَّل من القرن العشرين إلى القوى الاستعمارية على أنَّها عوامل تغييرٍ في الشرق الأوسط. مما يعني أن الحداثة كانت تقدِمةً من هذه القوى الأوروبية. على الرغم من أنَّه في العصر العثماني وتحديداً في أواخر القرن التاسع عشر وأوائل القرن العشرين تم استحداث التعليم الشامل، كما تطوَّرت مفاهيمٌ وأشكالٌ جديدةٌ للحياة العامة، حيث أصبحت الرياضة والأنشطة الترفيهيَّة الأخرى شائعةً خلال هذه الفترة. استمرت هذه الاتجاهات حتى ثلاثينيات القرن الماضي. طالب الطلابُ في مدينة حماة السلطات الفرنسية في العام ١٩٣٧م، إمَّا بإعادة افتتاح النادي الرياضي الذي أغلقته منذ العام ١٩٣٣ أو بتعيين مدرِّس تربيةٍ بدنيةٍ في مدرستهم، انطلاقاً من الشعور بأنَّ سوريا الجديدة تتطلَّب شباباً يتمتعون بلياقةٍ بدنيةٍ.

The Sarāyā Bridge with the Danish Expedition's house, Khān Rustm Bāshā, in the background
Photo: Ḥāmid al-Kīlānī, 1937?

جسر السرايا وفي الخلفية منزل البعثة الدنماركية «خان رستم باشا»
الصورة: حامد الكيلاني، عام ١٩٣٧

Looking west towards al-Dabāġa quarter in the southern part of the town, two hotels – rare in 1930s Hama – can be seen on either side of the bridge: the Nahr al-ʿAāṣī (Orontes) on the right, and the ʾAbī al-Fidā' on the left. Next to the Orontes Hotel, on the riverside, a covered outdoor café can be seen. This hotel played a significant role in the history of Syria, as it was here that there was a reception for the delegation from the National Bloc, having come from Paris with the Treaty of Independence in 1936. There was a beautiful view of the Orontes from the hotel, and speeches were delivered on official occasions and on holidays from its balcony.

In front of the ʾAbī al-Fidā' Hotel, work is underway to extend the cobblestone surface already on the bridge. The plazas and alleyways of Hama were characterized by a distinctive form of decorative cobblestone paving (Arabic *ġarzah*). The façade of the Khān Rustm Bāshā, the Danish Expedition's house from 1936 to 1938, can be seen at the end of the boulevard. The relatively modern buildings, like the hotels, in this part of town contrast greatly with those in the old parts of town.

عند النظر غرباً باتجاه حيّ الدبّاغة في الجزء الجنوبي من المدينة، يمكن رؤية فندقين على جانبي الجسر (وهو أمرٌ نادرٌ في حماة خلال الثلاثينيات): فندق نهر العاصي على الجهة اليمنى وفندق أبي الفداء على الجهة اليسرى والذي بُني كما هو مؤرخٌ عليه عام ١٩٣٣م. على ضفاف النهر، يمكن رؤية مقهىً خارجيٍّ مغطىً مجاوراً لفندق نهر العاصي. لهذا الفندق ذكرى جميلةٌ مع تاريخ سوريا حيث استقبل الفندق وفد الكتلة الوطنية قادماً من باريس وحاملاً معه معاهدة الاستقلال عام ١٩٣٦م. للفندق أيضاً اطلالةٌ جميلةٌ على نهر العاصي، حيث اتُخِذَ من شرفته منبراً لإلقاء الخُطب في المناسبات الرسميَّة والأعياد والاشراف على عروض الخيل والتجمُّعات الجماهيريَّة.
أمام فندق أبي الفداء، نلاحظ استكمال أعمال رصف الطريق والمنجز مسبقاً على الجسر، تميَّزتْ ساحات وأزقَّة حماة بأسلوبٍ مميزٍ في طريقة التبليط الذي سُمي بالغرزة، حيث يتم غرز ورصف الحجارة بطريقةٍ منتظمةٍ بالأسلوب الواضح في الصورة. في نهاية الشارع، يمكن رؤية واجهة خان رستم باشا، الذي خُصِّص كمنزلٍ للبعثة الدنماركية من عام ١٩٣٦ إلى عام ١٩٣٨م. تتناقض المباني الحديثة في هذا الجزء من المدينة بشكلٍ كبيرٍ، مثل الفنادق، مع تلك الموجودة في الأجزاء القديمة من المدينة.

View from the mound looking east at the river and al-Hadir quarter beyond
Photo: Mathilius Elo, 1931

Immediately below the mound is the Nūrī Mosque, built in 1162, and its associated waterwheels, al- Jābiryah and al-Ṣahyūniyah. The Shaykh Bridge can be seen entering the passageway through the Kīlānī Mansion.

منظرٌ من التلّ باتجاه الشرق للنهر وحي الحاضر خلفه
الصورة: ماتيليوس إيلو، عام ١٩٣١

أسفلُ التلّ مباشرةً يمكن رؤية مسجد النوري الذي بني عام ١١٦٢م والنواعير المرتبطة به «الجابرية والصهيونية». كما يظهر أيضاً جسر بيت الشيخ أو كما يطلق عليه أيضاً «جسر الكيلانية» وهو المعبر الوحيد الذي يخترق واجهة قصر الكيلاني.

Houses along the Orontes in the Bāb al-Jisr neighbourhood
Watercolour: Ejnar Fugmann, 1937

A scene illustrating how the town was built up along the banks of the river, ensuring a cool breeze from the water in the summer. Less clearly shown are women washing clothes on the edge of the river. Open riverbanks in the town were often occupied by women washing clothes, which posed a challenge for Ejnar Fugmann when he wanted to paint from the riverbank.

Fugmann, who painted this watercolour, was the chief architect for the entire length of the Expedition and published the Expedition's scientific report on the pre-Classical periods at Hama in 1958. He loved the exotic nature of the town of Hama and documented it in around 100 watercolours, about a third of which are in the National Museum of Denmark. Especially during the excavation seasons in 1931–33 and 1937–38, he could be found on his day off out in the town with his easel and paints.

منازلٌ بمحاذاة نهر العاصي في حي باب الجسر
لوحة مائيَّة: أينار فوجمان، عام ١٩٣٧

مشهدٌ يوضّح كيف تمَّ بناءُ المدينة على ضفاف النهر ممَّا يؤمِّن نسائم باردةٍ وعليلةٍ خلال فصل الصيف. يُظهِر المشهد بشكلٍ أقلَّ وضوحاً نساءً يغسلن الملابس على حافة النهر. غالباً ما كانت ضفاف الأنهار المفتوحة في المدن تشغلها نساءً يغسلن الملابس، الأمر الذي شكَّل تحدياً لأينار فوجمان عندما أراد الرسم من ضفة النهر.

كان فوجمان، منفِّذُ هذه اللوحة المائية، المهندس الرئيسي طوال مدَّة عمل البعثة الدنماركية، كما نشر أيضاً التقرير العلمي المتعلِّق بالفتراتِ ما قبل الكلاسيكية في حماة عام ١٩٥٨م. أحبَّ الطبيعة الغريبة لمدينة حماة ووثَّقها في حوالي مائة لوحةٍ مائيَّةٍ، ثُلثها تقريباً محفوظٌ في المتحف الوطني الدنماركي.

Members of the Danish Archaeological Expedition during the 1933 season
Photo: Hama Expedition, 1933

Director of the Expedition Harald Ingholt surrounded by staff. From left to right: Nora Scott, Ejnar Fugmann, Jørgen Rohweder, Poul Jørgen Riis, Frode Jensen, Florence Day, Bodil Hornemann (with hat), and Kubiak, a volunteer. The core members of the Expedition were the director Ingholt, architect Fugmann and conservator Jensen. Jensen came with experience from Shilo in Palestine and spoke Arabic. From 1932 onwards the team was joined by sculptor and Egyptologist Bodil Hornemann, who served as a photographer. Archaeologist Poul Jørgen Riis participated for four seasons, while Russian-born architect Georges Tchalenko spent three seasons at Hama. Over the years, the Danish team was thus composed of both aspiring and experienced archaeologists, architects, and conservators. This involvement at Hama forged strong bonds among the team members, many of whom remained life-long friends.

أعضاء البعثة الأثريَّة الدنماركية خلال موسم عام ١٩٣٣
الصورة: البعثة الدنماركية في حماة، عام ١٩٣٣

مدير البعثة الدنماركيية هارالد إنغولت محاطاً بأعضاء البعثة. من اليسار إلى اليمين: نورا سكوت، أينار فوجمان، يورغن روهويدر، بول يورغن ريس، فروذ ينسن، فلورنس داي، بوديل هورنمان، وكوبياك، متطوع. كان الأعضاء الأساسيين في البعثة هم المدير هارالد إنغولت والمهندس المعماري أينار فوجمان والمحافظ فروذ ينسن. هذا الأخير كان خبيراً في منطقة الشرق الأدنى نتيجة عمله مسبقاً في تلِّ شيلو (خربة سيلون) في فلسطين وكان يتحدث اللغة العربية أيضاً. اعتباراً من العام ١٩٢٣م، انضَّم إلى الفريق النحَّات وعالم المصريات بوديل هورنمان، الذي عَمِل كمصورٍ. شارك عالم الآثار بول يورغن ريس لمدة أربعة مواسم، بينما أمضى المهندس المعماري الروسي المَولد جورج تشالينكو ثلاثة مواسم في حماة. على مر السنين، كان الفريق الدنماركي يتألف من علماء الآثار والمهندسين المعماريين والمحافظين الطموحين وذوي الخبرة على حد سواء. تشكلت روابط صداقةٍ قويةٍ بين أعضاء الفريق العامل في حماة، كما ظلَّ الكثير منهم أصدقاء مدى الحياة.

Expedition members documenting the Great Mosque

Drawing: Ejnar Fugmann, 1933

Drawing of Poul Jørgen Riis (left) and Jørgen Rohweder (right) taking photos of the Great Mosque. Harald Ingholt stands in the centre with a local individual.

Fugmann drew a number of sketches of the work on the mound and scenes in the town, as well as activities in the Expedition house, and interactions between the Danes and locals. Here he depicts photos being taken from two directions of the Treasury (the elevated structure) in the courtyard of the Great Mosque. Although single reflex cameras using photographic film were available in the 1930s, the Danes seem to have depended on the plate camera depicted in the sketch. This form of camera used a glass plate negative; almost all of the negatives that are stored in the Hama Collection at the National Museum of Denmark are glass plate negatives.

أعضاء البعثة الدنماركية يوثِّقون الجامع الكبير في حماة

الرسم: أينار فوجمان، عام ١٩٣٣

في الرسم يَظهر بول يورغن ريس إلى اليسار ويورغن روهويدر إلى اليمين يلتقطان صوراً للجامع الكبير، بينما يتحدث هارالد إنغولت (في الوسط) إلى رجلٍ محلي.

بالإضافة إلى لوحاته بالألوان المائيَّة، رسم فوجمان أيضاً عدداً من الرسوم التخطيطيَّة (كروكي) وثَّق فيها العمل في التلِّ وفي المدينة، بالإضافة إلى مختلف الأنشطة ضمن منزل البعثة، وكذلك أيضاً العلاقات بين الدنماركيين والسكَّان المحليين.

في هذا الشكل على سبيل المثال يقوم فوجمان بتصوير مرحلة توثيق العمل ضمن الجامع الكبير في حماة وبشكلٍ خاص قبَّة الخزنة التي تقعُ في الجنوب الغربي من صحن الجامع الكبير. على الرغم من توفُّر آلات التصوير العاكسة الفردية التي تَستخدم أفلام التصوير الفوتوغرافي في الثلاثينيات، يبدو أنَّ الدنماركيين اعتمدوا على آلة التصوير اللوحيَّة الموضَّحة في الرسم التخطيطي. يعتمد هذا النوع من آلات التصوير على الألواح الجافة وهي عبارةٌ عن ألواحٍ زجاجيةٍ. تقريباً كل الصور المحفوظة في المتحف الوطني الدنماركي موثقةٌ بهذا النوع من الألواح الزجاجية.

ʿAẓm Palace. Reception for the Danish Expedition at the end of the first excavation season in 1931
Photo: al-Siūfī, a local photographer, 1931

Harald Ingholt sits in the foreground to the left, without a hat, with Ejnar Fugmann (wearing a hat) next to him. In the center of the front row of local dignitaries is Jamīl al-Bārūdī (in the white suit), and to his left is the special friend of the Expedition, Dr. Tawfīq al-Shīshaklī.

The local Syrian dignitaries are almost all dressed in the standard Ottoman attire of the upper and middle classes, a Western suit and the Ottoman fez (Arabic *ṭarbūsh*). The older men would have been educated in institutions of higher learning in Damascus or Istanbul established in late Ottoman times, or at universities in Europe. They are also all likely to have served in the Ottoman army during the First World War. These are the type of men who led the movements of national liberation in the Post-Ottoman Middle East. Until the mid-19th century, headgear, especially, served as an identity marker – ethnicity, religion, rank – but the empire-wide adoption of the fez (and western clothes) replaced these individual markers of identity with a shared identity as an Ottoman bureaucrat and notable by people of diverse ethnic and religious backgrounds. These changes were not adopted, or were even actively rejected, by conservative urban artisans and tradesmen, as well as folk in the countryside. Atatürk had already banned the fez in 1925 in his campaign to westernize Turkey. However, in Syria political identity was chiefly anti-colonial, framed by continued attachments to familiar Ottoman forms.

قصر العظم. حفل استقبال البعثة الدنماركية في نهاية موسم التنقيب الأول عام ١٩٣١
الصورة: السيوفي، عام ١٩٣١

يجلس هارالد إنغولت في المقدِّمة إلى اليسار، وبجانبه أينار فوجمان (يرتدي قبعة). في وسط الصف الأمامي من الشخصيات المحلية، جمِيل البارودي (بالبدلة البيضاء)، وإلى يساره الصديق المقرَّب للبعثة الدنماركية، الدكتور توفيق الشيشكلي.

في أقصى اليمين في الصف الأمامي يوجد ضابطٌ فرنسي، وإلى اليسار كاهنٌ من طائفةِ الروم الأرثوذكس، وعددٌ من رجال الدين المسلمين. كان الرجال من كبارِ السنّ في حماة في ذلك الوقت قد تلقّوا تعليمهم في مؤسسات التعليم العالي في دمشق أو اسطنبول التي تأسَّست في أواخر العهد العثماني، أو في جامعات أوروبا. كان من رجالات هذه الحقبة العديد من اللذين قادوا حركات التحرُّر الوطني في الشرق الأوسط ما بعد العهد العثماني.

من خلال الصورة، يرتدي جميعُ الشخصيات السورية المحليَّة المرموقة الزي العثماني التقليدي للطبقات العليا والمتوسِّطة، والمتمثل بالبدلة الغربيَّة والطربوش العثماني (الطربوش العربي). اعتاد أن يُغطي جميع الرجال في الشرق الأوسط رؤوسهم في الأماكن العامة في هذا الوقت، حتى منتصف القرن التاسع عشر كانت أغطية الرأس، على وجه الخصوص، بمثابة علامة هويَّةٍ للدين والمرتبة الاجتماعية. فيما بعد تبنَّت الإمبراطورية العثمانية الطربوش على نطاقٍ واسعٍ واعتبرته زياً رسمياً، فأصبح جميع موظفي الدولة والضباط العسكريين يلبسون الطربوش الأحمر باعتباره كهويةٍ مشتركةٍ. لم يتم اعتماد هذه التغييرات، أو حتى تم رفضها فعلياً، من قبل الحرفيين والتجار المحافظين في المناطق الحضريَّة، كما في مناطق الأرياف. ومع ذلك، كانت الهويَّة السياسيَّة في سوريا مناهضةً للاستعمار بشكلٍ أساسي، وقد تمَّ تأطيرُها من خلال الارتباط المستمر بالأشكالِ العثمانية المألوفة في ذلك الوقت.

Khān Rustm Bāshā courtyard

Watercolour: Ejnar Fugmann, 1937

The Expedition house was an old caravansary built in 1561. The courtyard would originally have held the pack animals and trade goods transported by merchants travelling the "Sultanic Road" north and south through the Ottoman Empire. In the centre of the courtyard is a small mosque.

Ejnar Fugmann appears to have favoured architecture when choosing a motif for his watercolours – perhaps not surprising, given his training as an architect. He had a tendency to leave out modern "intrusions" on and around the Ottoman buildings, giving the places he depicted a sense of tranquility that may not have always characterized the place in actuality. If people were included, one gets the impression they were mainly there for scale. The buildings themselves were depicted carefully and precisely, and the watercolours provide a rare opportunity to view 1930s Hama in colour.

فناء خان رستم باشا

لوحة مائية: أينار فوجمان، عام ١٩٣٧

كان منزل البعثة الدنماركية عبارةً عن خانٍ قديمٍ تمَّ بناؤه عام ١٥٦١م (بناه رستم باشا في عصر السلطان سليمان القانوني). ضمن فناء هذا الخان كان يتمُّ الاحتفاظ بالمواشي والدواب بالإضافة إلى السلع التجاريَّة التي ينقلها التجَّار الذين يسافرون على الطريق السلطاني شمالاً وجنوباً عبر الإمبراطورية العثمانية.

فضَّل أينار فوجمان المباني الهندسيَّة لتنفيذ لوحاته بالألوان المائيَّة، وهو ربما ليس بالأمر المستغرب، بالنظر إلى كونه مهندساً معمارياً. كان يميل إلى استبعاد «التدخُّلات» الحديثة في المباني العثمانية وما حولها، ممَّا أعطى الأماكن التي صورها احساساً بالهدوء الذي ربما لم يكن يَعكِس واقعَ الحال دائماً. تمَّ تصوير المباني نفسها بعنايةٍ ودقةٍ، وتُوفِّر الألوان المائيَّة فرصةً نادرةً لمشاهدة مدينة حماة بالألوان خلال ثلاثينيات القرن الماضي.

ويونانُ حلّتْ في الرحابِ وبعدها   لرومةَ مجدٌ في حماكِ مكينُ
ومن ثمّ عمّتكِ المهابةُ والهدى   بجيشِ بني عدنانَ فيكِ قطينُ
همُ الأسدُ في يومِ الوغى يستفزّهمْ   لخوضِ المنايا الدائراتِ يقينُ
لهمْ من تعاليمِ النبيّ «محمّدٍ»   سلاحٌ له الشوسُ الكماةُ تدينُ

... ...

مضتْ حقبٌ والدارُ تعفو رسومُها   ويعلو رُباها وحشةٌ وسكونُ
وفي تُربِها سرُّ الحياةِ محجّبٌ   وكنزٌ من العلمِ الصحيحِ ثمينُ
عجبتُ لقومي يعظمون جدودَهمْ   وتاريخهمْ تحتَ الترابِ دفينُ
يجيئهمُ من نازحِ الغربِ جهبذٌ   عليمٌ بنيلِ المكرماتِ قمينُ
يسائلُ في الربعِ المحيلِ حجارةً   جماداً فتبدي سرَّها وتبينُ
ويدخلُ في بحرِ الترابِ شراعُهُ   وفورُ حجاهُ والثباتُ سفينُ
لكَ الخيرُ يا انكولت نقّبْ عنِ الأُلى   تفانوا وحدّثْ فالحديثُ شجونُ
فكمْ في ثرانا من مليكٍ ممنّعٍ   ومن أسدٍ لم يحتبسْه عرينُ

وكم من حكيمٍ كان ملءَ زمانِهِ   يُحلّي مقاماتِ النهى ويَزينُ
وكم من خطيبٍ بل وكم من مغرّدٍ   يجيبه صوتٌ لديهِ حنونُ
هنالكَ في مهدِ البلى مستقرّه   وآثارُهمْ في المستراد كمونُ
إذا بلغَ التنقيبُ منكَ رفاتَهم   فمهلاً عليها فالكريمُ يصونُ
ولا تُزهق الأجدادَ في غفلاتِهمْ   فإنّكَ بالمجدِ التليدِ ضنينُ
سيذكركَ التاريخُ ذكراً مخلّداً   وتحويكَ منهُ كتبُ النبوغِ بطونُ

حماه : «بدر الدين الحامد»

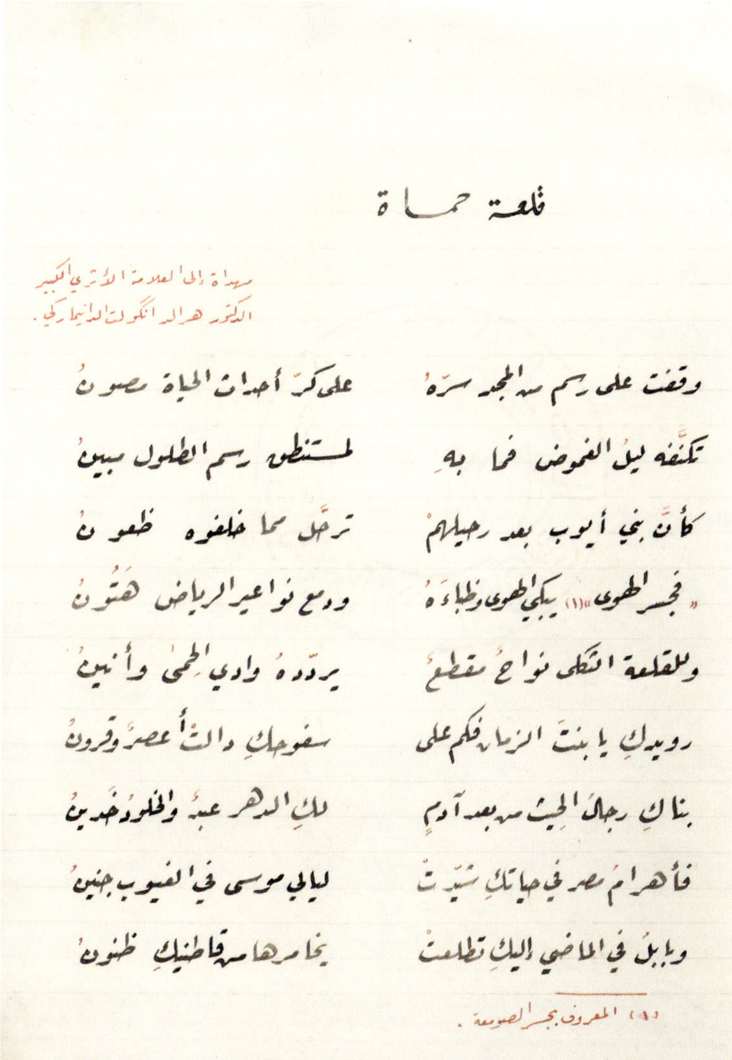
قلعة حماة

مهداة إلى العلامة الأثري الكبير
الدكتور هارالد انكولت الدانماركي.

وقفت على رسم سما المجد سره — على كر أحداث الحياة مصون
تكنفه ليل الغموض فما به — لمستنطق رسم الطلول مبين
كأن بني أيوب بعد رحيلهم — ترحل مما خلفوه ظعون
بجسر الطوى (١) يبكي الطوى وظباءه — ودمع نواعير الرياض هتون
وللقلعة الثكلى نواح مقطع — يردده وادي الحمى وأنين
رويدك يا بنت الزمان فكم على — سفوحك ذات أعصر وقرون
بناك رجال الحث من بعد آدم — لك الدهر عبد والخلود خدين
فأهرام مصر في حياتك شيدت — ليالي موسى في الغيوب جنين
وبابل في الماضي إليك تطلعت — يخامرها من قاطنيك ظنون

(١) المعروف بجسر الصومعة.

Poem written for Harald Ingholt by Badr al-Dīn al-Ḥāmid

Poem by the famous Syrian poet Badr al-Dīn al-Ḥāmid. Handwritten, presumably by the poet himself, and previously unpublished. Entitled "The Citadel of Hama", the poem was recited by al-Ḥāmid at a reception held by the Danish Expedition.

The poem describes the long history of Hama and its citadel ("here before the Pyramids") and the ongoing excavations. In the poem, al-Ḥāmid thanks Ingholt for bringing the history of the city to light, and reminds him to look after both its ancestors and its heritage with care and respect.

Badr al-Dīn al-Ḥāmid (1899–1961) was born into an important Sufi family in Hama, where he studied religious sciences and Arabic. He was nicknamed the poet of al-ʻAāṣī (Orontes). He was skilled in reciting poetry and was a member of the Literary Club in Hama, founded in 1922, where he recited his poems in public. His poetry is of both a patriotic and a mystical character. He published his first collection of poetry in 1928, as well as a theatrical play, "Maysalūn", in Hama in 1946.

Al-Ḥāmid took part in the national movements of the time. He was a member of the National Bloc and a close friend of Tawfiq al-Shīshaklī; the political and social developments in Syria, and in Hama in particular, are reflected in his poetry, which forms part of the Syrian school curriculum.

قصيدةٌ كتبها الشاعر بدر الدين الحامد مهداةٌ لمدير البعثة الدنماركية هارالد إنغولت

ارشيف البعثة الدنماركية في حماة

قصيدةٌ للشاعر السوري بدر الدين الحامد. مكتوبةٌ بخطِّ اليد، على الأرجح من قبل الشاعرِ نفسهِ، ولم تُنشر من قبل. بعنوان «قلعة حماة»، تلاها الحامد وأهداها لهارالد إنغولت في حفل استقبالٍ أقامته البعثة الدنماركية. تصف القصيدة التاريخ الطويل لمدينة حماة وقلعتها، وأعمال التنقيب الجارية. في القصيدة يشكر الحامد إنغولت على إبراز تاريخ المدينة، ويذكِّره بالعناية والاحترام بتراثها وأسلافها.

وُلِدَ الشاعر بدر الدين الحامد وعاش في مدينة حماة بين الأعوام ١٨٩٩ و١٩٦١م من أسرةٍ أكثرُ رجالها من المشتغلين بالعلم والأدب، تأثَّر بوالده الشيخ محمود الحامد الذي كان أحَد أقطابِ المذهب الصوفيّ في مدينة حماة حيث درس على يديه العلوم الدينية واللغة العربية. لُقِّب بدر الدين الحامد بشاعر العاصي، كان بارعاً في إلقاء الشعر ويدين بمعظم نتاجه الأدبي إلى النادي الأدبي في حماة الذي أُسِّس سنة ١٩٢٢م، حيث كان يُلقي قصائده على الملأ. شارك في الحركات الوطنيَّة وكان من رجالات الكتلة الوطنيَّة وكان وصديقاً مقرباً لتوفيق الشيشكلي. تتقاسم موضوعاته الشعرَ الوطنيّ، القوميّ، الشعر الصوفي وشعر الغزل. أصدر ديوانه الأول عام ١٩٢٨م، ثم مسرحيته الشعرية «ميسلون» في حماة عام ١٩٤٦م. تنعكس التطورات السياسيَّة والاجتماعيَّة في سوريا، وحماة على وجه الخصوص، في شعره الذي يشكِّل جزءً من المناهج المدرسيَّة السوريَّة.

The Hama Expedition workforce in the first season, 1931
Photo: al-Siūfī, 1931

During the 1930s, large workforces with relatively little supervision were commonplace on archaeological excavations in the Middle East. There could be up to 400 workmen at one time digging in the large excavation unit in the centre of the mound at Hama. In the Expedition house, local staff served as conservators, working with Frode Jensen. A number of locals were also responsible for daily maintenance and housekeeping. During this period there was ordinarily a clear distinction between the Western archaeologists and the local workforce; however, the Danish team seems to have forged close bonds with their local workmen. Even though they brought in experienced Egyptian foremen, there were also local foremen over the years. The workers were also overseen by a member of the powerful Kīlānī family (in the right foreground in the photo – wearing the fez and three-piece suit).

العمَّال المشاركين في الموسم الأول للتنقيب مع البعثة الأثريَّة الدنماركية عام ١٩٣١
الصورة: السيوفي، عام ١٩٣١

خلال الثلاثينيات من القرن الماضي، كان من المألوفِ جداً مشاركةُ أعدادٍ كبيرةٍ من العمَّال المحليين في الحفريات الأثريَّة في مختلف مناطق الشرق الأوسط. في بعض الأحيان كان العدد يَصِلُ إلى أكثر من أربعمائة عامل يعملون في وقتٍ واحدٍ ضمن قطاعٍ واحدٍ كبيرٍ في مركز التلِّ الأثري. في منزل البعثة في حماة، عَمِلَ بعض الأشخاص المحليين كمرممين مع المرمّم المختص فروذ ينسن. كما كان عددٌ من الأشخاص مسؤولين عن أعمال الصيانة اليوميَّة والتدبير المنزلي.

خلال تلك الفترة من الزمن كان هناك عادةُ تمييزٍ واضحٍ بين علماء الآثار الغربيين والقوى العاملة المحليَّة. ومع ذلك، يبدو أن الفريق الدنماركي قد أقام روابط وثيقة مع عمَّالهم المحليين. بالرغم من أنهم اعتمدوا على رؤساء عمَّالٍ مصريين ذوي خبرةٍ، كان هناك أيضاً رؤساء عمَّالٍ محليين على مرِّ السنين. كان المشرف على العمَّال خلال أعمال التنقيب في حماة أحدُ أعضاء عائلة الكيلاني الكبيرة والمعروفة في المدينة (في مقدمة الصورة من الجهة اليمنى - يرتدي الطربوش).

The bathhouse Hammam al-Darwīshiyah

Drawing: Ejnar Fugmann, 1935

In addition to his watercolours and sketches, Fugmann also drew scale-drawings of particular structures in town. These include, in addition to the public baths illustrated here, the Expedition house, Khān Rustm Bāshā, and the largest of the water-wheels, al-Muḥamadyah. Although the drawing is not labelled, our sources suggest that this is the al-Darwīshiyah Hammam built in the 1570s, located in a small square not far from Khān Rustm Bāshā. This was one of Fugmann's favorite parts of town and, probably not coincidentally, the baths that his friend Dr. Shīshaklī frequented.

حمَّام الدرويشيَّة

الرسم: أينار فوجمان، عام ١٩٣٥

بالإضافة إلى ورسوماته ولوحاته بالألوان المائيَّة، قام فوجمان أيضاً بعملية الرفْع الهندسي لبعض المباني في المدينة. وتشمُل هذه المباني، حمَّام الدرويشيَّة الموضَّح هنا في هذا الشكل، بيت البعثة الدنماركية «خان رستم باشا»، ناعورةُ المحمدية، أكبر نواعير حماة وأقدمها. على الرغم من عدم تسمية الرسم، تشير مصادرنا إلى أنه حمَّام الدرويشيَّة، والذي بُني في سبعينيات القرن السادس عشر، ويقعُ في ساحةٍ صغيرةٍ ليست ببعيدةٍ عن خان رستم باشا. كانت هذه واحدةٌ من الأحياء المفضَّلة لفوجمان ضمن مدينة حماة، وربما ليس من قبيل الصدفة، فقد كان من الأحياء والحمامات التي يرتادها صديقه الدكتور الشيشكلي.

A
B
C

Mathilius Elo working on restoring the Hama Lion
Photo: "Klingen" art magazine, 1942

Mathilius Schack Elo served as the conservator on the excavation for a single season, in 1931. He was a sculptor and worked as a conservator at the art museum Ny Carlsberg Glyptotek in Copenhagen. He was responsible for restoring the Hama Lion, the most complete and spectacular of the gate guardian figures that were found in the Iron Age citadel. Since 1999, the lion has been on exhibit as a long-term loan in the Archaeological Museum in Hama. Most of the photographs in the Hama Collection at the National Museum of Denmark are of the excavations and of the architectural fabric of the surrounding town. The only photographs in the Collection that record daily life in town and in the surrounding countryside are those taken by Elo in 1931.

ماتيليوس إيلو يعمل على ترميم أسد حماة الآرامي
مجلة «كلينغن» الفنية، عام ١٩٤٢

عَمِل ماتيليوس شاك إيلو كمرمِّمٍ للبعثة الدنماركية لمدّة موسمٍ واحدٍ في عام ١٩٣١م. كان نحاتاً وعمل محافظاً في متحف كارلسبرغ غليبتوتيك في كوبنهاغن. كان مسؤولاً عن ترميم أسد حماة، أروع وأكمل تماثيل حرّاس البوابة التي عُثر عليها في قلعة العصر الآرامي. يُعرَض الأسد حالياً في المتحف الوطني في حماة كإعارة طويلة الأمد منذ عام ١٩٩٩م. كان إيلو الظاهر في الصورة الوحيد من بين أعضاء الفريق الدنماركي الذين وثّقوا الحياة اليومية في مدينة حماة والمناطق الريفية المحيطة بها من خلال الصور التي التقطها في عام ١٩٣١م.

Courtyard of the Great Mosque, with orchards in the background
Photo: Hama Expedition

The Great Mosque was built in the 7th century. However, this was the site of sacred buildings stretching back to at least the mid-3rd century CE, when first a Roman temple and then a Christian church occupied the location. It was supplied with water from the largest waterwheel at Hama, al-Muḥamadyah, which can be seen in the background to the left.

This was the principal mosque in a town that already in the 1930s was a stronghold of religious conservatism. As we shall see, Hama was one of the centres of the Syrian struggle against French Mandatory rule; for many, this represented a struggle of Islam against the invading Christian infidel.

فناء الجامع الكبير في حماة مع بساتينه في الخلفية
الصورة: البعثة الدنماركية في حماة

تمَّ بناء الجامع الكبير في القرن السابع الميلادي، ويُعتبر أعظم آبدةٍ عمرانيَّةٍ باقيةٍ في مدينة حماة، وقد بدأ هذا الجامع كمعبدٍ روماني، ثم أضحى كنيسةً كبرى في العهد البيزنطي. كان هذا المكان موقعاً للمباني المقدَّسة منذ منتصف القرن الثالث الميلادي على أقل تقدير. تم امداده بالمياه عن طريق أكبر نواعير المدينة «المُحمدية» والتي يمكن رؤيتها في خلفيَّة الصورة إلى اليسار.
خلال ثلاثينيات القرن الماضي كان الجامع الكبير الجامع الرئيسي في مدينة حماة، كما كان أيضاً معقلًا للمحافظين الدينيين. كما سنرى لاحقاً، كانت حماة أحد مراكز النضال السوري ضد حكم الانتداب الفرنسي. بالنسبة للكثيرين في ذلك الوقت، كان هذا يمثِّل صراع الإسلام ضدَّ الغزاة المسيحيين.

Fugmann's watercolour of the courtyard in the Great Mosque

Watercolour: Ejnar Fugmann, 1938

Courtyard with treasury, prayer hall and southeast minaret. The late 8th century octagonal raised treasury building is unusual, only found in two other places: in the Umayyad Mosque in Damascus, and al-'Aqṣā Mosque complex in Jerusalem.

لوحة لفوغمان بالألوان المائيَّة لفناء الجامع الكبير

لوحة مائية: أينار فوجمان، عام ١٩٣٨

نرى في اللوحة صحن الجامع مع قبَّة الخزنة، المُصلى والمئذنة الجنوبية مربعة الشكل. بنيت قبَّة الخزنة في أواخر القرن الثامن، وقد أُقيمت على ثمانية أعمدةٍ اسطوانيةٍ لها تيجانٌ كورنثية. لا يوجد لها مثيلٌ إلا في المسجد الأموي بدمشق، وبجوار المسجد الأقصى في القدس.

Courtyard of the Great Mosque
Photo: Hama Expedition, 1932

Ejnar Fugmann's attention to detail in his watercolours is confirmed by this photo from nearly the same spot as the previous illustration. The scene here, though, is livelier than that in the watercolour.

فناءُ الجامع الكبير
الصورة: البعثة الدنماركية في حماة، عام ١٩٣٣

هذه الصورة تُظهِر اهتمام أينار فوجمان بأدقّ التفاصيل عند تنفيذ لوحاته بالألوان المائيَّة، الصورة مأخوذةٌ تقريباً من نفس مكان اللوحة السابقة. ومع ذلك، فإن المشهد في الصورة هنا يبقى أكثر حيويَّةٍ من ذلك الموجود على لوحة الألوان المائيِّة.

58 Bro over Orontesfloden. Paa arabisk hedder Floden El-'Aṣi. Til venstre nogle af de store Vandhjul.

The Bayt Al-Shaykh Bridge between the Nūrī Mosque and the Kīlānī Mansion

Watercolour: Charles Christensen, 1931

The view is towards the north, with the Nūrī Mosque to the left and the Kīlānī Mansion on the right, connected by the Bayt Al-Shaykh Bridge crossing the Orontes. The mound can be seen in the background; Christensen noted on the margins of the watercolour that the figures on the mound were women enjoying the view.

Charles Christensen served as an architect for the first season only, in 1931. He took part in surveys and renovations of historical buildings in Denmark and was employed in the Medieval Department at the National Museum. His are the only other watercolours known from the time of the Expedition apart from Fugmann's.

جسر بيت الشيخ بين جامع النوري وقصر الكيلاني

لوحة مائيَّة: تشارلز كريستنسن، عام ١٩٣١

منظرٌ باتجاه الشمال، يظهر فيه مسجد النوري إلى اليسار وقصر الكيلاني إلى اليمين، يصل فيما بينهما جسر بيت الشيخ (جسر الكيلانية)، بينما يظهر في الخلفية تلّ حماة؛ أشار كريستنسن إلى أنَّ الشخصيات الموجودة على التلّ كانت من النساء اللواتي يتمتعن بمشاهدة المدينة من أعلى التلّ.

عمل تشارلز كريستنسن كمهندس معماري للموسم الأول فقط (عام ١٩٣١). شارك في عمليات المسوحات وإعادة تأهيل المباني التاريخية في الدنمارك وعمل في قسم العصور الوسطى في المتحف الوطني الدنماركي. لوحاته من الألوان المائيَّة هي الوحيدة الأخرى المعروفة من حماة خلال ثلاثينيات القرن الماضي باستثناء لوحات فوجمان.

'Aẓm Palace *ḥaramlik*

Photo: Hama Expedition, 1932?

The 'Aẓm Palace was originally built in 1742 by 'As'ad Bāshā al-'Aẓm, who later became governor of Damascus. Viewed here is the *ḥaramlik*, the family quarters, of the 'Aẓm Palace, situated on top of the more public ground-level areas that would have included, among other things, the Palace storerooms. Since 1956, the Palace has served as a museum of folk traditions.

The 'Aẓm Palace was rebuilt and expanded until the decline of the family's fortunes. The 'Aẓm's were one of several notable families in Hama who had risen to power during Ottoman times. Although it was not impossible for "new men" to rise in Ottoman Syria, the status of one's family was the most important indicator of rank. At the top were the land-holding families, who also usually held high positions in the Ottoman bureaucracy. These families also sometimes engaged in large-scale business ventures. Below this class, a middle position was occupied by ordinary merchants, bankers, and money-lenders. Small shopkeepers and government clerks formed an even lower level of this middle rank. These indicators of status remained in place in Syria into the 1930s.

قصر العظم «الحرملك»

الصورة: البعثة الدنماركية في حماة، عام ١٩٣٢؟

يعتبرُ قصر العظم من أجمل الأوابد العمرانيَّة العائدة للعصر العثماني في حماة، أول من بناه هو أسعد باشا العظم عام ١٧٤٢م الذي أصبح فيما بعد حاكم دمشق. في الصورة نشاهد قسم الحرملك، القسم الخاص بالحريم والعائلة والواقع في الجناح الجنوبي للقصر. يشغل القصر منذ عام ١٩٥٦م مقر متحف التقاليد الشعبية، بعد أن بقي حتى منتصف السبعينيات متحف المدينة الرئيسي. أُعيد بناء قصر العظم وتوسيعه على مدى القرون التالية حتى تدهورت ثروات العائلة. كانت عائلة العظم واحدةً من عدة عائلاتٍ بارزةٍ في حماة والتي صَعِدت إلى السلطة خلال العهد العثماني.

على الرغم من أنَّه لم يكن من المستحيل على «الرجال الجدد» الارتقاء في الدولة والمجتمع في سوريا العثمانية، إلا أنَّ منزلة الأسرة كانت أهم مؤشرٍ على مكانة ورتبة العائلة. على رأس القائمة كانت العائلات المالكة للأراضي، وهي التي تتقلَّد أيضاً أعلى المناصب الإدارية، كما شاركت هذه العائلات أحياناً في مشاريعٍ تجاريةٍ واسعة النطاق. بالدرجة الثانية، احتل التجَّار العاديون والمصرفيون ومقرضو الأموال مركزًا متوسطاً. فيما شكَّل أصحاب المتاجر الصغيرة والموظفون الحكوميون مستوىً أدنى في تركيبة المجتمع. ظلَّت مؤشرات الوضع هذه قائمةٌ في سوريا حتى الثلاثينيات من القرن الماضي.

ʻAẓm Palace *al-Qāʻa*

Photo: Bodil Hornemann? 1938

قاعة الاستقبال في قصر العظم

الصورة: بوديل هورنمان، عام ١٩٣٨

Inside the ʻAẓm Palace, the *qāʻa*, reception room, featured a small fountain under an elaborately decorated dome. Ornate reception rooms like this in palatial mansions were often embellished with a combination of stones of alternating colour, mosaics, and stalactite vaulting that supported a dome. Intricately carved wooden doors and panels added to the grandeur.

تُعدُّ هذه القاعة من أجمل القاعات الأثريَّة، إن لم تكن أجملها في المشرق العربي. غالباً ما كانت غرف الاستقبال المتقنة في القصور الفخمة مزيَّنةً بأسلوبٍ قائمٍ على مبدأي التناظر والتنويع، سواء أكان في رصف الأحجار ذات الألوان المتناوبة، أو في زخرفة الأبواب والنوافذ والكوَّات العلوية المنحوتة بشكلٍ معقَّدٍ والتي تُضفي عنصر الفخامة إلى المكان. تتألَّف القاعة من الداخل من عتبةٍ تتوسطها نافورة ماءٍ جميلةٍ من الرخام والحجارة الملونة، وتعلوها قبَّةٌ واسعةٌ تضمُّ بين حناياها زوايا حجريَّة غنية بالمقرنصات والمتدليات.

‘Aẓm Palace courtyard

Photo: Hama Expedition, 1938

During the 1930s the ‘Aẓm Palace was used as a school. The photographer has captured a group of school boys in what appears to be a break between classes.

باحة قصر العظم

الصورة: البعثة الدنماركية في حماة، عام ١٩٣٨

خلال الثلاثينيات من القرن الماضي، كان قصر العظم يُستخدم كمدرسةٍ. التقط المصوِّر في هذه الصورة مجموعةً من طلاَّب المدارس فيما يبدو أنَّه استراحةٌ بين الفصول الدراسيَّة.

'Aẓm Palace courtyard

Watercolour: Ejnar Fugmann, 1938?

With the 'Aẓm Palace presented here in colour, we can now fully appreciate the typical Ottoman overhanging extension of the upper floor, here painted blue. School boys are standing in groups in the courtyard, and one of them is playing with one of the spigots of the fountain.

باحة قصر العظم

اللوحة المائيَّة: يِنار فوجمان، عام ١٩٣٨

مع عرض قصر العظم هنا بالألوان، تُمكِّننا هذه اللوحة من تقدير الامتداد المتدلّي للطابق العلوي النموذجي للطراز العثماني والمطلي باللون الأزرق. في المشهد، يقف طلاَّب المدرسة في مجموعاتٍ ضمن الباحة، وأحدهم يلعب بأحد صنابير النافورة.

'Aẓm Palace fountain spigot

Photo: Bodil Hornemann, 1938

Close-up of the elaborate spigot.

نافورة ماء، قصر العظم

الصورة: بوديل هورنمان، عام ١٩٣٨

لقطةٌ مقرَّبةٌ لصنبور الماء متقن الصنع.

The Bayt Al-Shaykh Bridge leading through the Kīlānī Mansion
Photo: Hama Expedition

A view across the river from the Nūrī Mosque, whose water-wheels can be seen on the left of the photo. A low dam had been built across the river to direct the water towards the water-wheels.

The Kīlānī Mansion is really a complex of buildings built in different periods, the earliest of which dates to the 13th century, while most of the rest date to the 17th and 18th centuries. The mansion itself was built in 1715 and renovated in 1781. Although the ʿAẓm family, mentioned above, had lost some prestige by the 1930s, the Kīlānī family continued to be a powerful force in Hama. This retention of status was at least partly due to the fact that the Kīlānīs claimed descent from the Prophet and, therefore, held the paramount religious positions in town. This whole area of the town of the 1930s no longer exists.

جسر بيت الشيخ المؤدي إلى قصر الكيلاني
الصورة: البعثة الدنماركية في حماة

منظرٌ عبر النهر من مسجد النوري حيث يمكن رؤية ناعورته المائية على يسار الصورة. في هذه النقطة تمَّ بناء سدٍ منخفضٍ عبر النهر لتوجيه المياه نحو النواعير. يبدأ حي الكيلانية بالجسر الوحيد الذي يصله بالضفة الغربية للنهر الذي يُطلُّ بواجهاته على النهر مباشرةً، القصر عبارةٌ عن مجمَّعٍ من المباني التي تمَّ بناؤها في فتراتٍ مختلفةٍ، يعود أقدمها إلى القرن الثالث عشر بينما يعود تاريخ البقيَّة إلى القرنين السابع عشر والثامن عشر. تمَّ بناء القصر نفسه عام ١٧١٥م وتم تجديده عام ١٨٧١م. على الرغم من أنَّ عائلة العظم، المذكورة أعلاه، قد فَقدت بعض هيبتها بحلول الثلاثينيات، إلا أنَّ عائلة الكيلاني استمرت في كونها قوةً كبيرةً في مدينة حماة. كان هذا الاحتفاظ بالمكانة العائلية يرجع جزئياً على الأقلِّ إلى حقيقة أنَّ عائلة الكيلاني زعموا أنَّهم ينحدرون من نسل النبي، وبالتالي احتلوا المناصب الدينية العليا في المدينة. تجدُر الإشارة هنا إلى أنَّ المنطقة بأكملها من المدينة لم تعد موجودة اليوم.

Street view
Photo: Mathilius Elo, 1931

Although this photo is not labelled, we may be looking at the road that continued from the Bayt al-Shaykh Bridge through the Kīlānī Mansion complex.

The polarization of classes in Hama was the most extreme of any area in Syria in the 1930s. Political power in Hama was held by just four families. The status of the ʿAẓm and Kīlānī families had been established already by the 18th century (with influential branches in Damascus), while the Barāzī and Ṭaīfūr families joined this elite group in the early 19th century. The exalted position of these families resulted from their ownership of large estates and their monopoly of the highest bureaucratic and religious offices in town. Their control of the town and the surrounding countryside was almost absolute: the four families owned almost all of the over 100 villages in the countryside around Hama.

منظرٌ لأحد شوارع حماة
الصورة: ماتيليوس إيلو، عام ١٩٣١

على الرغم من عدم تسمية هذه الصورة، لكن نعتقد أنَّ الصورة مأخوذةٌ ضمن مجمَّع قصر الكيلاني.

كان الاستقطاب الطبقي في حماة هو الأكثر تطرفاً من أي منطقةٍ أخرى في سوريا خلال الثلاثينيات وكانت السلطة السياسية في حماة تقع تحت سيطرة أربع عائلاتٍ فقط. ترسَّخت مكانة عائلتي العظم والكيلاني بقوةٍ في مدينة حماة في القرن الثامن عشر، بينما انضمت عائلتا برازي وطيفور إلى هذه النخبة في أوائل القرن التاسع عشر. احتكرت هذه العوائل أعلى المناصب السياسيَّة والدينيَّة في المدينة، بالإضافة إلى امتلاكهم لأكبر العقارات في حماة. سيطروا بشكلٍ شبه مطلقٍ على المدينة والريف: امتلكت العائلات الأربع ما يزيد عن مائة قريةٍ تقريباً في ريف حماة.

Kīlānī Mansion seen from across the river

Watercolour: Charles Christensen, 1931

The Kīlānī Mansion was situated directly on the Orontes across from the Nuri Mosque, with its own waterwheel to supply the complex with water.

قصر الكيلاني يُرى من الجانب الآخر للنهر

اللوحة المائيَّة: تشارلز كريستنسن، عام ١٩٣١

كان قصر الكيلاني يقعُ مباشرةً على نهر العاصي على الجانب المقابل لجامع النوري، في الصورة نرى ناعورة المياه التي خصِّصت لتزويد المجمَّع بالمياه.

Khān Rustm Bāshā courtyard

Photo: Poul Jørgen Riis, 1937

View towards the north over the Khān Rustm Bāshā, with the shops across the street from the Khān visible along al-Murābiṭ Street. The mound is in the far distance. Visible in the Khān is the back of the entrance façade, the upper floor of which served as the living quarters for members of the Expedition. The small building in the centre of the courtyard had served as a mosque for travellers staying at the caravansary.

باحة خان رستم باشا

الصورة: بول يورغن ريس، عام ١٩٣٧

منظرٌ باتجاه الشمال من فوق خان رستم باشا، حيث تَظهرُ المحلات التجاريَّة المقابلة للخان على طول شارع المرابط، كما يمكننا رؤية تلِّ حماة الأثري في الأفق. ضمن الخان يظهر القسم الخلفي من واجهة المدخل، حيث خُصِّص الطابق العلوي منه كسكنٍ لأفراد البعثة الدنماركية. يتوسط باحة الخان مبنى صغير هو عبارةٌ عن مسجدٍ خُصِّص للمسافرين المقيمين في الخان.

The façade of the entranceway into Khān Rustm Bāshā
Photo: Hama Expedition
Watercolour: Ejnar Fugmann, 1932

As noted earlier, Hama was located on the "Sultanic Road" in Ottoman times. This was the major north-south communications route through the Levant, and caravansaries were placed along this route at regular intervals to service the caravan trade. By the 1930s, however, caravan trade had declined in importance due to the rise of the railroad and automobile, and many caravansaries had gone out of use. Khān Rustm Bāshā was built in 1561 by al-Sayed Rustm Bāshā during the reign of the Ottoman Sultan Suleiman the Magnificent. It served as the Expedition house from 1936 to 1938 and later served as an orphanage.

The juxtaposition of the photograph with Fugmann's watercolour illustrates his tendency to romanticize the old town in his paintings. He has dispensed with the rubble in the street, the telephone lines, signpost, and posters plastered on the façade of the caravansary visible in the photograph.

واجهة مدخل خان رستم باشا

الصورة: البعثة الدنماركية في حماة

اللوحة المائيَّة: أينار فوجمان، عام ١٩٣٢

كما أشرنا سابقاً، كانت حماة تقعُ على «الطريق السلطانية» في العهد العثماني، وهو الطريق الرئيسي في بلاد الشام الذي يربط الشمال بالجنوب. انتشرت خاناتُ القوافل على طول هذا الطريق بطريقةٍ منتظمةٍ، وهي عبارةٌ عن مضافاتٍ أو نزلٍ كبيرة صُمِّمت لاستقبال التجار المسافرين وقوافلهم أثناء عبورهم لهذه الطرق. بحلول الثلاثينيات من القرن الماضي، تراجعت أهمية تجارة القوافل بسبب صعود دور السكك الحديديَّة والسيارات، وبهذه الطريقة خرجت معظم خانات القوافل عن الخدمة.

بُني الخان عام ١٥٦١م على يد رستم باشا في عهد السلطان العثماني سليمان القانوني. استُخدم بين الأعوام ١٩٣٨ و١٩٣٦م كمنزلٍ للبعثة الأثريَّة الدنماركية، ثم أصبح لاحقاً داراً للأيتام.

تسمح لنا مقارنةُ الصورة مع اللوحة المائيَّة بتوضيح ميل فوجمان إلى إضفاء الطابع الرومانسي على المدينة القديمة في لوحاته، لقد استغنى عن الأنقاض الموجودة في الشارع وخطوط الهاتف واللافتات والملصقات الظاهرة في الصورة.

The Nūrī Mosque
Photo: al-Siūfī, 1931

This mosque was built in 1162 by the great Zengid ruler, Nūr al-Dīn, a potent enemy of the Second Crusade. The two water-wheels – al-Jābiryah and al-Ṣahyūniyah – supplied water to the mosque and to the cisterns of nearby houses in the Bāshūra district. In the background, figures can be seen excavating the buildings of the Iron Age citadel on the southern edge of the mound.

جامع النوري
الصورة: السيوفي، عام ١٩٣١

يعود تاريخ بناء جامع النوري لعام ١١٦٢م، من قبل السلطان نور الدين الزنكي (العدو القوي للحملة الصليبية الثانية)، وهو يعتبر أهمَّ آبدةٍ معماريَّةٍ تعود للعهد الزنكي. زُوّد الجامع بالمياه عن طريق نواعير الجعبرية والصهيونية (الواضحة في الصورة) والتي زَوَّدت بدورها خزاناتُ المنازل المجاورة ضمن حي الباشورة بالمياه. في خلفيَّة الصورة، يمكن رؤية بعض الأشخاص الذين يقومون بالتنقيب عن مباني قلعة العصر الآرامي على حافَّة التلِّ من الجهة الجنوبية.

Al-Jābiryah and al-Ṣahyūniyah Waterwheels

Watercolour: Ejnar Fugmann, 1932

A close-up of the waterwheels seen from the Bāshūra neighbourhood looking towards the Kīlānī Mansion and the Shaykh Bridge.

ناعورة الجعبرية وناعورة الصهيونية (الصاهونية)

اللوحة المائيَّة: أينار فوجمان، عام ١٩٣٢

لقطةٌ مقرَّبةٌ للنواعير التي تُرى من حي الباشورة وهي تُطلّ باتجاه قصر الكيلاني وجسر بيت الشيخ.

Al-Jisriyah Waterwheel
Photo: Ḥāmid al-Kīlānī

The waterwheel is viewed from the east, towards the Sarāyā Bridge. The waterwheels that line the river in Hama remain the town's most iconic elements. These wooden waterwheels are said to be the most beautiful ever built. They were needed to transfer water from the deeply cut river onto the attached aqueducts, or other channeling systems, which provided water for facilities in town and for the nearby gardens and orchards. The river current moved the wheel, and buckets on the wheel picked up water from the river and emptied it into the channel of the aqueduct. Schedules regulated access to the water so that it could be shared. It is not known when the first waterwheels were built at Hama. Although it is thought that waterwheels existed already by the late Roman Period, a Byzantine mosaic at the nearby site of Apamea, dating to 469 CE, is the first real evidence for their existence. According to the medieval writer Yāqūt (ca.1225), there were several waterwheels in Hama already around 884 CE. There were about 20 waterwheels in Hama in the 1930s when the Danish archaeologists were excavating on the mound, and most of them still exist.

ناعورة الجسريَّة
الصورة: حامد الكيلاني

صورةٌ لناعورة الجسريَّة من الشرق باتجاه جسر السرايا. تُعتبر نواعير حماة المائيَّة التي تصطفُّ على ضفاف نهر العاصي من أهمِّ وأشهر الأوابد الأثريَّة في المدينة ويُقال عنها أروع نواعير خشبيةٍ تمَّ بناؤها على الإطلاق. كان الهدف منها حملُ الماء إلى مستوىً أعلى من مستوى النهر نظراً لانخفاض مجرى نهر العاصي في أراضي حماة عن مستوى الحوض الذي ينسابُ فيه.
عن كيفية عملها: يدور الدولاب الخشبي للناعورة بقوة التيار المائي للنهر، أثناء دورانها تَغطس الناعورة بالماء لتمتلئ صناديقها المثبَّتة على محيط الناعورة بماء النهر، التي بدورها تنقل المياه إلى حوضٍ علوي ومنه يجري في قنواتٍ محملَّةٍ على قناطر لتسقي بها المدينة وبساتينها، ومن أجل ذلك وضعت جداولٌ دقيقةٌ جداً من أجل تقاسُمِ المياه. لا يُعرف متى تمَّ بناء أول ناعورة في حماة. على الرغم من أنَّه يُعتقد أنَّ النواعير كانت موجودةٌ بالفعل في أواخر العصر الروماني، إلا أنَّ الفسيفساء البيزنطية التي عُثِرَ عليها في موقع أفاميا القريب من حماة، والتي يعود تاريخها إلى٤٦٩م، هي أوَّل دليلٍ حقيقي على وجودها. وفقاً لكاتب العصور الوسطى ياقوت الحموي (حوالي ١٢٢٥م)، كان هناك العديد من النواعير في حماة حوالي عام ٨٨٤ م. خلال ثلاثينيات القرن الماضي وثَّق الدنماركيون أثناء أعمال التنقيب في التلِّ حوالي ٢٠ ناعورة، لا يزال معظمها موجوداً حتى يومنا هذا.

Ma'mūriyah Waterwheel and men working in foreground
Photo: Hama Expedition

This waterwheel, situated in the Bāshūra neighbourhood and one of the oldest in Hama, dates to 1453.

ناعورةُ المأموريَّة وبعض الرجال يعملون في النهر
الصورة: البعثة الدنماركية في حماة

تقعُ الناعورة في حي الباشورة، كانت تسمَّى الناعورة الكبيرة وتعتبر ثاني أكبر ناعورةٍ في حماة بعد ناعورة المحمديَّة وأقدمها، يوجد على برجها كتابةٌ تدلُّ على انشائها من قبل الأمير بلباك في عام ١٤٥٣م.

Ma'mūriyah Waterwheel

Watercolour: Ejnar Fugmann, 1932

A view of the waterwheel from the Sarāyā Bridge. Note how the dam helps direct, and increase the speed of, the water stream towards the wheel. There is an inscription on the stone support for the waterwheel that proclaims its construction by Prince Balbak in 1453.

ناعورة المأموريَّة

اللوحة المائيَّة: أينار فوجمان، عام ١٩٣٢

منظرٌ للناعورة من جسر السرايا. نلاحظ كيف ساعد السدُ في توجيه وزيادة سرعة تدفُّق المياه نحو الناعورة.

The Dahshah Waterwheel north of the mound
Photo: Hama Expedition

The identity of the two individuals in the photo is not known, although the figure on the horse may be Jørgen Rohweder, a member of the Danish Expedition. As we have emphasized, the Danish archaeologists were entranced by the old town and the river that ran through it, punctuated by the spectacular wooden waterwheels with their stone aqueducts. As individuals who were interested in the past, they were naturally drawn to the picturesque elements of the urban landscape around the mound they were excavating. However, there were powerful political and social undercurrents beneath the tranquil scenes documented by the Danes in the 1930s, which they did not capture in photographs and other media.

ناعورة الدهشة شمال تلِّ حماة
الصورة: البعثة الدنماركية في حماة

هوية الشخصين في الصورة غير معروفةٍ، نعتقد أن الشخص الذي يمتطي الحصان هو يورغن روهويدر، عضو في البعثة الدنماركية. كما أكدنا سابقاً، فإن علماء الآثار الدنماركيين كانوا مفتونين بالمدينة القديمة وبنهر العاصي الذي كان يمرُّ عبرها، وبشكلٍ خاصٍ بنواعيرها الخشبيَّة المذهلة وقنواتها الحجريَّة. كباحثين مهتمين بالماضي، انجذبوا بشكلٍ طبيعيٍ إلى المعالم الخلابة المنتشرة حول التلِّ الذي كانوا ينقِّبون فيه. أَخفتْ هذه المشاهد الهادئة التي وثَّقها الدنماركيون في الثلاثينيات من القرن الماضي، استقطاباتٍ سياسيةٍ واجتماعيةٍ حادةٍ لم تَلتقِطُها عدسات الكاميرات ووسائل الإعلام الأخرى.

Dr. Tawfīq al-Shīshaklī (1884–1940)
Photo: Hama Expedition
Photo of pin: National Museum of Denmark

Above, a pin of the Hama chapter of the National Bloc political organization, belonging to Dr. Shīshaklī, who gave it to Poul Jørgen Riis, a member of the Danish Expedition. It is now in the collection of the National Museum of Denmark, donated by Thomas Riis. Dr. Shīshaklī was a member of one of the lesser notable families in Hama. He studied at the Ottoman Medical Academy in Istanbul before joining the Ottoman army as a doctor in 1914. During the First World War, he served as a surgeon at the Military Hospital in Medina, in what is now Saudi Arabia. After the war he returned to Hama and opened an eye clinic. In 1928 he co-founded *al-Kutla al-Waṭanīah*, the National Bloc political party (along with its president, Hāshim al-'Atāsī), and served in the parliament in the 1930s. The aim of the National Bloc was to create a free, democratic and secular Syrian republic. Unlike most of his colleagues in the National Bloc, Dr. Shīshaklī held socialist views and promoted the improvement of living conditions in rural districts. In fact, for the most part, the National Bloc only represented a very small, elite segment of Syrian society. Members were the sons of wealthy landowners, merchants, or bureaucrats. These men and their families had all benefited politically and economically under both Ottoman and French rule and were in the main unwilling to drastically change the economic and social status quo.

د. توفيق الشيشكلي (١٨٨٤-١٩٤٠)
الصورة: البعثة الدنماركية في حماة
صورة الدبوس: المتحف الوطني الدنماركي

في الصورة أعلاه دبوسٌ يحمل شعار فرع حماة لتنظيم الكتلة الوطنية السياسيَّة، يعود للدكتور الشيشكلي، الذي سلَّمه إلى بول يورغن ريس، عضو البعثة الدنماركية، وهو الآن محفوظٌ ضمن مجموعة المتحف الوطني الدنماركي، بعد أن تبرع به توماس ريس للمتحف.
ينحدر الدكتور الشيشكلي من أفراد إحدى العائلات الأقل شهرة في حماة، نشأ وترعرع فيها ثم انتسب إلى المدرسة الطبية العثمانية في اسطنبول وتخرَّج منها طبيباً عام ١١٩١م، قبل أن يلتحق بالجيش العثماني كطبيبٍ عام ١٩١٤م. خلال الحرب العالميَّة الأولى، تم تعينه ضابطاً طبيباً في المشفى العسكري في المدينة المنورة، بعد الحرب عاد إلى حماة وافتتح عيادةً متخصِّصةً في طبِّ العيون. ساهم مع بعض وجوه وأعيان حماة في تأسيس الكتلة الوطنية (إلى جانب رئيسها هاشم الأتاسي) في دمشق عام ١٩٢٨م، وكان رئيساً لفرع الكتلة في حماة، كما عمل في البرلمان خلال الثلاثينيات. كان هدف الكتلة الوطنية إنشاء جمهوريَّةٍ سوريَّةٍ حرَّةٍ وديمقراطيةٍ وعلمانيةٍ. على عكس معظم زملائه في الكتلة الوطنيَّة، كان للدكتور الشيشكلي آراء اشتراكيةٍ وروَّج لتحسين الظروف المعيشيَّة في المناطق الريفيَّة. في الواقع، لم تُمثِّل الكتلة الوطنية في الجزء الأكبر منها سوى شريحة نخبويَّة صغيرة جداً من المجتمع السوري. كان أعضاء الكتلة من أبناء ملاكي الأراضي الأثرياء أو التجار أو البيروقراطيين. استفاد هؤلاء الرجال وعائلاتهم جميعاً سياسياً واقتصادياً في ظلِّ الحكم العثماني والفرنسي وكانوا في الغالب غير مستعدين لتغيير الوضع الاقتصادي والاجتماعي الراهن بشكل جذري.

Expedition members with Syrian friends

Photo: Hama Expedition, 1932

Expedition members and friends in the first Expedition house in 1932. The house belonged to the ʿAẓm family, and was located in the Bāshūra quarter along the Orontes. In the center of the photo is Ingholt, to his left Tawfīq al-Shīshaklī, and behind them, Khuḍir al-Shīshaklī. To Dr. Shīshaklī's left is Fugmann, followed by Dueholm and Rohweder; to Ingholt's right, down the stairs, Jamīl al-Bārūdī in the tan suit, then Bodil Hornemann, who took most of the photographs of the excavation, and ʿAbd al-Raḥman al-Shīshaklī, father of Tawfīq. From the upper left in descending order: Frode Jensen, Vagn Poulsen (an archaeology student and later the director of the Ny Carlsberg Glyptotek Museum) and Poul Jørgen Riis.

Dr. Shīshaklī was a great friend and supporter of the Danish Expedition. He formed deep friendships with Harald Ingholt, Ejnar Fugmann, and other members of the Danish team. In fact, by the 1930s the colonial authorities were not the only faction in Mandatory Syria that used archaeology for political purposes. Syrian Nationalists, such as Shīshaklī and other members of the National Bloc, had begun to use archaeology in their own campaign for the territorial integrity of a "Greater Syria" not bounded by the borders imposed by the French. Syrian Nationalists emphasized secularism rather than Islam in their vision of a future Syrian state and so celebrated the achievements of the pre-Islamic civilizations as a basis for national pride. The friendship between the Danes and Syrians such as Shīshaklī is likely to have been strengthened by this common interest in Syria's deep past.

أعضاء البعثة الدنماركية مع أصدقاء سوريين

الصورة: البعثة الدنماركية في حماة، عام ١٩٣٢

أعضاءُ البعثة الدنماركية وأصدقائهم في أوَّل منزلٍ للبعثة عام ١٩٢٣. يعود المنزل لعائلة العظم، ويقع في حي الباشورة على طول نهر العاصي. في وسط الصورة يقف إنغولت، وإلى يساره توفيق الشيشكلي وخلفهما خضر الشيشكلي. على يسار الدكتور الشيشكلي يقف فوجمان، يليه ديوهولم وروهويدر، على يمين إنغولت، أسفل الدرج، جميل البارودي بالبدلة البيضاء، ثم بوديل هورنمان، الذي التقط معظم صور أعمال التنقيب، وعبد الرحمن آغا الشيشكلي، والد توفيق. من أعلى اليسار بترتيبٍ تنازلي: فروذ ينسن، فاجن بولسن (ولاحقاً مدير متحف كارلسبرغ غليبتوتيك) وبول يورغن ريس.

كان الدكتور الشيشكلي صديقاً حميماً وداعماً للبعثة الدنماركية. كوَّن صداقاتٍ متينةٍ وعميقةٍ مع هارالد إنغولت وأينار فوجمان وأعضاء آخرين من الفريق الدنماركي. في الواقع، بحلول الثلاثينيات من القرن الماضي، لم تكن السلطات الاستعماريَّة الفصيل الوحيد في سوريا الانتدابية الذي استخدم علم الآثار لأغراضٍ سياسيةٍ. بدأ القوميون السوريون، مثل توفيق الشيشكلي وأعضاء آخرين في الكتلة الوطنيَّة، في استخدام علم الآثار في حملتهم الخاصة من أجل وحدة أراضي «سوريا الكبرى» غير المحدودة بالحدود التي فرضها الفرنسيون. أكد القوميون السوريون على العلمانية بدلاً من الإسلام في رؤيتهم لدولة سورية المستقبليَّة واحتفلوا بإنجازات حضارات ما قبل الإسلام كأساس للاعتزاز الوطني، ولا سيما الحضارات الفينيقية وبلاد ما بين النهرين والحضارة الرومانيَّة. من المحتمل أن تكون الصداقة التي تشكَّلت بين الدنماركيين والسوريين أمثال الشيشكلي قد تعزَّزت من خلال هذه المصلحة المشتركة في التاريخ العميق لسوريا.

Tawfiq al-Shīshaklī reading the Franco-Syrian Treaty
Photo: Postcard, Hama Expediton, 1936

توفيق الشيشكلي يقرأ المعاهدة الفرنسيَّة السوريَّة
الصورة: بطاقة بريدية البعثة الدنماركية في حماة، عام ١٩٣٦

Dr. Tawfīq al-Shīshaklī reads the Franco-Syrian Treaty over the microphone to an assembled crowd in Hama, 1936. The Treaty, negotiated by members of the National Bloc, was an official recognition of Syrian independence (which, in fact, was not realized until 1946). Dr. Shīshaklī is joined by other notables to his right, with his fellow deputy from Hama, Najīb Bey al-Barāzī at his side. Muslim clerics view the proceedings from inside the building behind Shīshaklī.

With the spread of education beginning already in the early years of the 20th century, along with the increased circulation of a popular press, political awareness in Hama spread beyond the elite classes. A professional middle class developed that was younger and more radical than most members of the Syrian Nationalists in the National Bloc, and unlike the traditional elite that accounted for most members of the National Bloc, this new, younger group campaigned for social and economic justice. It also rejected the National Bloc's reliance on pre-Islamic achievements to legitimize its struggle against the French, forming an Arab Nationalist faction that privileged the achievements of its Arab heritage.

الدكتور توفيق الشيشكلي يقرأ المعاهدة الفرنسية السورية على الملأ أمام حشدٍ من النَّاس في حماة عام ١٩٣٦م. كانت المعاهدة، التي تفاوض عليها أعضاء الكتلة الوطنية، بمثابة اعترافٍ رسميٍ باستقلال سوريا (والذي لم يتحقق في الواقع حتى عام ١٩٤٦م). في الصورة، ينضمُّ إلى الدكتور الشيشكلي وجهاء آخرون من حماة، إلى يمينه زميله ونائبه نجيب بك البرازي. فيما يقف رجال دينٍ مسلمون يتابعون الإجراءات من داخل المبنى الواقع خلف الشيشكلي.

مع انتشار التعليم الذي بدأ بالفعل في السنوات الأولى من القرن العشرين، إلى جانب الانتشار المتزايد للصحافة الشعبية، انتشر الوعي السياسي في حماة خارج طبقات النخبة. نتيجةً لذلك تطوَّرت طبقةٌ وسطى أصغر سناً وأكثر راديكالية من معظم الأعضاء القوميين السوريين في الكتلة الوطنية، وعلى عكس النُخبة التقليديَّة التي تُمثِّل معظم أعضاء الكتلة الوطنية، قامت هذه المجموعة الجديدة الشابة بحملاتٍ من أجل تحقيق العدالة الاجتماعيَّة والاقتصاديَّة. كما رفضت اعتماد الكتلة الوطنيَّة على إنجازات ما قبل الإسلام لإضفاء الشرعيَّة على نضالها ضد الفرنسيين.

Opening of the Syrian Parliament in Damascus
Photo: Postcard, Hama Expediton, 1936?

Fāris al-Khūrī speaks to members of the Syrian Parliament. A long-time statesman, Khūrī became Prime Minister of Syria from 1944 to 1945, and again from 1954 to 1955. He represented Syria as one of the founding members at the inauguration of the United Nations in 1945. Dr. Shīshaklī is seated to the left on the dais, as the first Parliament Secretary. To the right, Nāẓim al-Qudsī, a Syrian politician, who later (1961–63) served as President of Syria.

Although the Syrian Nationalists and Arab Nationalist factions were often able to work together against the French, they increasingly were at odds about the identity of a post-colonial Syria. The Syrian Nationalist elite mainly campaigned against the borders of Syria imposed by the French; however, they also repressed the importance of an Arabic and Islamic foundation for the identity of a future Syrian state, emphasizing instead the prioritization of a shared Syrian identity based on its ancient past. The Arab Nationalists, on the other hand, focused on the achievements from the beginning of the Islamic period onwards that tied the Arab world together, and the glories of the early Islamic periods, such as the Umayyad and Abbasid Caliphates. The approach of the pan-Arab Nationalists eventually triumphed over that of the Syrian Nationalists.

جلسة افتتاح البرلمان السوري في دمشق
الصورة: بطاقة بريدية البعثة الدنماركية في حماة، عام ١٩٣٦

فارس الخوري يتحدَّث إلى أعضاء البرلمان السوري. كان الخوري زعيماً وطنياً سورياً وأحد الآباء المؤسسين للجمهوريَّة السوريَّة. تسلَّم رئاسة البرلمان السوري ثم رئاسة الوزراء في الثلاثينيات والأربعينيات، ليعود رئيساً للحكومة في عهد الاستقلال سنة ١٩٥٤م. مثَّل سوريا كأحد الأعضاء المؤسسين في افتتاح الأمم المتحدة عام ١٩٤٥م. في الصورة يجلس الدكتور الشيشكلي إلى اليسار على المنصة كأوَّل سكرتيرٍ لمجلس النوَّاب. إلى اليمين، ناظم القدسي، سياسيٌّ سوريٌّ تولَّى فيما بعد (١٩٦٣-١٩٦١م) رئاسة سوريا.
على الرغم من أنَّ القوميين السوريين والفصائل القوميَّة العربيَّة كانوا غالباً قادرين على العمل معاً ضدَّ الفرنسيين، إلا أنَّهم كانوا على خلافٍ متزايدٍ بشأن هويَّة سوريا ما بعد الانتداب. قامت النخبة القوميَّة السوريَّة بشكلٍ أساسيٍ بحملةٍ ضدَّ الحدود الجغرافيَّة التي فرضها الفرنسيون. ومع ذلك، فقد قاموا أيضاً بقمع هوية الدولة السوريَّة المستقبليَّة القائمة على_الأساس العربي والإسلامي، وشدَّدوا بدلاً من ذلك على إعطاء الأولويَّة للهويَّة السوريَّة المشتركة على أساس ماضيها القديم. من ناحيةٍ أخرى، ركز القوميون العرب على انجازات العصر الإسلامي وما بعده والتي ربطت العالم العربي معاً، كما اعتمدوا في نهجهم على أمجاد الفترات الإسلامية المبكِّرة، مثل الخلافة الأمويَّة والعباسيَّة. في نهاية المطاف انتصر نهج القوميين العرب على نهج القوميين السوريين.

A square in the Jūrat Ḥawā quarter
Photo: Hama Expedition

The square is lined with shops and cafés; to the left is a public bath. Note the stack of stools in the middle of the square, ready to be used by the patrons of the coffee shop to the right. In front of the photographer, a boy carries what look like milk jugs.

Cafés, where men gathered to drink coffee, smoke water pipes, and read newspapers, became increasingly popular as locations for patriotic theatrical presentations. Of the 50 to 60 cafés in Hama at this time, one of the largest was owned by Tawfīq al-Shīshaklī. It was famous for these types of theatre productions, often performed by younger members of the notable families. Neither the colonial authorities nor the more conservative elements in town approved of these performances.

The standard Ottoman notable "uniform" of fez and three-piece suit are not seen here and in the following photos of public spaces and marketplaces in the old town. This feature seems to illustrate the situation, noted earlier, in which urban shopkeepers and working-class men, along with rural folk, retained costumes that proclaimed their individual identity.

ساحةٌ في حيّ جورة حوّا

الصورة: البعثة الدنماركية في حماة

تعجُّ السَّاحة بالمحلات التجارية والمقاهي، ونلاحظ أيضا وجود حمامٍ عامٍ إلى اليسار من الصورة. في الوسط نلاحظ تكُدس الكراسي الخشبيَّة الصغيرة والجاهزة لاستقبال زبائن المقهى الموجود على يمين الصورة. أمام المصوِّر يقف صبيٌّ يحمل ما يشبه أباريق باعة الحليب.

أضحت المقاهي، حيث كان يجتمع الرجال لشرب القهوة وتدخين النرجيلة وقراءة الصحف، ذاتَ شعبيةٍ متزايدةٍ كمواقع للعروض المسرحيَّة الوطنيَّة في ثلاثينات القرن الماضي. كانت حماة في ذلك الوقت تضمُّ ما بين الخمسين إلى الستين مقهى، كان أحد أكبرها مملوكاً لتوفيق الشيشكلي. اشتهرت المقاهي بهذا النوع من الإنتاج المسرحي، وغالباً ما كان يؤديها أفرادٌ صغار السنِّ من العائلات البارزة. لم توافق السلطات الاستعماريَّة ولا حتى العناصر الأكثر محافظةً في المدينة على هذه العروض المسرحيَّة.

Murābiṭ Street seen from Fugmann's room in Khān Rustm Bāshā

Watercolour: Ejnar Fugmann, 1938

The Expedition house was situated in the 'Alīlīāt neighbourhood. Like all fountains, the one seen here was provided with water by one of the waterwheels, in this case the Jisriyah, which also supplied the water for Khān Rustm Bāshā. Fugmann has included the most common kinds of transportation in the town: donkeys and horse carts, the bicycle probably being more unusual.

شارع المُرابط من غرفة فوجمان في خان رستم باشا

اللوحة المائيَّة: أينار فوجمان، عام ١٩٣٨

يقعُ منزل البعثة الدنماركية في حي العليليَّات. مثل جميع النوافير في حماة، كانت النوافير التي نراها هنا تُزوَّد بالمياه عن طريق النواعير، في هذا الحي زَوَّدت ناعورة الجسرية الساحة وخان رستم باشا بالمياه. ضمَّن فوجمان في هذه اللوحة أكثر أنواع النقل شيوعاً في المدينة: الحمير وعربات الخيول، والدرَّاجة الهوائية التي تبدو أكثر غرابةً.

Hama 1/5.38
Ejnar Fugmann

Hama 1934
Soûq el Medineh
E. Fugmann

Sūq al-Medina

Watercolour: Ejnar Fugmann, 1934

A small square in Bāb al-Qiblī, west of the Great Mosque. As elsewhere in town, shade is provided by awnings and the narrow nature of the streets. On a roof terrace, vines have been planted for additional shade. Like in many houses in Hama, some of the windows are decorated with intricate lattice patterns to let the breeze in while at the same time inhibiting prying eyes.

سوق المدينة القديمة

اللوحة المائيَّة: أينار فوجمان، عام ١٩٣٤

ساحةٌ صغيرةٌ في حي باب القبلي غربي الجامع الكبير. كما هو الحال في أيّ مكانٍ آخر في المدينة، تمَّ توفير الظلّ من خلال الشوارع الضيِّقة والمظلّات الشمسيَّة الكبيرة. على شرفة السطح، زُرِعَتْ الكروم للحصول على المزيد من الظلِّ. كما هو الحال في العديد من المنازل في حماة، تمَّ تزيين بعض النوافذ بزخارف معقدةٍ بحيث تسمح بدخول نسائم الهواء وفي نفس الوقت تُجنِّب أعين المتطفلين من اختلاس النظر.

Street scene in a market place
Photo: Mathilius Elo, 1931

A busy scene in a market place in the old town, with Bedouin and local townspeople. As we have emphasized elsewhere, the Danish archaeologists seemed to have loved the exotic – to them – nature of both the place and the populace, and so they naturally documented these facets of 1930s Hama. And, while we feel that these types of photographs did not express any form of a sense of superiority, they do work – presumably inadvertently – in an allochronic way. That is, photographs of this period often served a narrative that depicted the inhabitants of Syria as stuck in the past, unable to embrace modernity without the help of the West, and unable to govern themselves.

مشهدٌ من الشارع في ساحة السوق
الصورة: ماتيليوس إيلو، عام ١٩٣١

مشهدٌ مزدحمٌ في أحَد الأسواق في المدينة القديمة، يظهر فيها سكَّان المدينة المحليين مع البدو. كما أكدنا في مكانٍ آخر، يبدو أنَّ علماء الآثار الدنماركيين قد أحبّوا الطَّبيعة الغريبة للمكان والسكَّان على حدٍ سواء، ولذا قاموا بشكل طبيعي بتوثيق هذه الجوانب من ثلاثينيات القرن الماضي في حماة. وبينما نشعرُ أنَّ هذه الأنواع من الصور لم تُعبِّر عن أي شكلٍ من أشكال الشعور بالتفوّق، فإنَّها تعمل، على الأرجح عن غير قصدٍ، بطريقة عكسيةٍ، أي أنَّ صور هذه الفترة غالباً ما خدمتْ سردية تصوُّر سكَّان سوريا على أنَّهم عالقون في الماضي، وغير قادرين على احتضان الحداثة دون مساعدة الغرب، كما أنَّهم غير قادرين على حُكم أنفسهم.

Narrow, winding alleyway in the old part of town
Watercolour: Ejnar Fugmann, 1932

In the Jūrat Ḥawā neighbourhood, a typically narrow alleyway with houses and a mosque with a simple overhanging minaret. This alley was crossed by the archaeologists on their way from the Expedition house at Khān Rustm Bāshā to the mound. From the evidence of their excavations, we know that the ancient town of Hama on the mound had equally narrow, winding streets in tightly packed neighbourhoods.

زقاقٌ ضيّقٌ ومتعرجٌ في الجزء القديم من المدينة
اللوحة المائيَّة: أينار فوجمان، عام ١٩٣٢

في اللوحة زقاقٌ ضيقٌ نموذجي ضمن حيّ جورة حوّا، حيث نرى بعض المنازل وجامعٌ بمئذنةٍ بسيطةٍ متدليةٍ. اعتاد علماء الآثار على اجتياز هذا الزقاق في طريقهم من منزل البعثة الأثريَّة في خان رستم باشا إلى التلِّ. نَعْلَمُ من خلال الحفريات التي قاموا بها، أنَّ مدينة حماة القديمة على التلِّ كانت هي أيضاً ضيقةً بنفس القدر مع شوارع متعرجةٍ ضمن أحياء مكتظةٍ بإحكام.

Hama 1982

Boy on donkey

Photo: Mathilius Elo, 1931

A busy market area; brooms are being sold in the background.

صبيٌّ على حمارٍ

الصورة: ماتيليوس إيلو، عام ١٩٣١

منطقة سوقٍ مزدحمةٍ؛ تباع المكانس في الخلفيَّة «مكانس القش».

An ironmonger's shop
Photo: Mathilius Elo, 1931

Ironmongers at work; a possible customer stands in front of the shop with what seems to be a lamb or small goat carcass. Various male names have been scribbled across the door.

In addition to campaigns for independence that crossed class boundaries, one particular stratum of Syrian society also fought for social justice. The artisanal-worker class began to press for higher wages, better working conditions, and the right to strike. Unions (*niqābat*) were formed and strikes called throughout the 1930s. The Communist Party of Syria and Lebanon played an important role in organizing workers. The French mandatory authorities and the traditional elite that made up the National Bloc were largely hostile to these perceived political threats and challenges to the inequality in Syrian society. Of course, there were exceptions among the elite, who did support social justice, like Dr. Shīshaklī, for instance.

متجرٌ للحدادة
الصورة: ماتيليوس إيلو، عام ١٩٣١

في الصورة الحدَّاد أثناء عمله، يقف زبونٌ محتملٌ أمام المحل ومعه ما يبدو أنَّه ذبيحةٌ لخاروفٍ صغيرٍ أو ماعزٍ. على الباب تمَّ تدوين أسماءٍ مختلفةٍ من الذكور.

قاتلت طبقةٌ معينةٌ من المجتمع السوري من أجل العدالة الاجتماعية، بالإضافة إلى حملات الاستقلال التي تجاوزت الحدود الطبقيَّة. بدأت طبقة العمَّال الحرفيين في الضغط من أجل رفع الأجور وتحسين ظروف العمل والحق في الإضراب. تمَّ تشكيل النقابات وتمَّت الدعوة إلى الإضرابات طوال ثلاثينيات القرن الماضي. لَعِبَ الحزب الشيوعي في سوريا ولبنان دوراً مهماً في تنظيم العمَّال. كانت سلطات الانتداب الفرنسي والنُّخبة التقليديَّة التي شكَّلت الكتلة الوطنية معاديةً إلى حدٍ كبيرٍ لهذه التهديدات والتحديَّات السياسيَّة لعدم المساواة في المجتمع السوري. بالطبع، كانت هناك استثناءاتٌ بين النخبة التي دعمت العدالة الاجتماعيَّة، مثل الدكتور الشيشكلي على سبيل المثال.

A wheelwright's shop
Photo: Mathilius Elo, 1931

As elsewhere in Syria in the 1920s and 30s, craftsmen and small shopkeepers in Hama were increasingly forced into conditions of poverty because they could not compete with the European products that began to inundate the market. A local notable, Abd al-Ḥamīd Qunbāz, formed a number of unions among the craftsmen and small shopkeepers of his town already by the late 1920s. Increasingly, in the 1930s, strikes and other forms of social unrest led to reprisals by the authorities. In 1936, 40 demonstrators were killed by government troops in the streets of Hama and martial law was declared. An article in the newspaper, *al-'Ayām* (Days) on the 27th of February, 1936, under the headline "Hama Still Under a General Strike", describes how Ingholt was so saddened that his friend Dr. Shīshaklī, who was ill, had been thrown in jail in connection with the strike that he traveled to Beirut to appeal to the French authorities to free his friend. However, when he returned to Hama with the release order, Dr. Shīshaklī, in solidarity with his fellow political prisoners, refused to be freed.

Al-'Ayām was one of the main Syrian newspapers that had been established during the Mandatory Period. It was founded by a member of the National Bloc.

متجرُ صانع العجلات
الصورة: ماتيليوس إيلو، عام ١٩٣١

كما هو الحال في أي مكانٍ آخر في سوريا في عشرينيات وثلاثينيات القرن الماضي، أُجبِر الحرفيون وأصحاب المتاجر الصغيرة في حماة على العيش في ظروفٍ من الفقر لأنَّهم لم يتمكَّنوا من منافسة المنتجات الأوروبية التي بدأت تُغرِق الأسواق. بحلول أواخر عشرينيات القرن الماضي أنشأ عبد الحميد قنباز «أحد الوجهاء المحليين البارزين» عددًا من النقابات للحرفيين وأصحاب المتاجر الصغيرة في حماة. أدت الإضرابات وغيرها من أشكال الاضطرابات الاجتماعيَّة، في الثلاثينيات من القرن الماضي، إلى أعمالٍ انتقاميَّةٍ من قبل السلطات. في عام ١٩٣٦، قُتِل أربعين متظاهراً على يد القوات الحكومية في حماة كما أُعلِنَت الأحكام العرفيَّة.

في السابع والعشرين من شهر شباط عام ١٩٣٦ عنونت جريدة «الأيَّام» مقالاً بعنوان «ما تزال حماة في اضرابها الشامل. الشيشكلي يرفض الخروج، دون غيره، من السجن» تحدَّث المقال بشكلٍ خاصٍ عن تأثُّر إنغولت (مدير البعثة الدنماركية) من سجن صديقه الدكتور توفيق الشيشكلي لأنَّه كان مريضاً حين سيق إلى سجن «الشرفة» في حماة، فسافر إلى بيروت خصيصاً لهذه القضية، وقد رَجِع ومعه قرارٌ بأخلاء سبيل الدكتور من سجنه وعندما عَرَضَ قائد السجن هذا القرار على الدكتور أجابه قائلاً: أنَّني لن أخرج من السَّجن حتى يخرج آخر سجينٍ، وظلَّ بالرغم من مرضه الشديد داخل السَّجن.

كانت صحيفة الأيَّام من أهم الصحف السوريَّة التي ظهرت في عهد الانتداب، والتي أُصدِرت من قبل أبرز شخصيات الكتلة الوطنيَّة.

A bakery
Photo: Mathilius Elo, 1931

The sign on the door proclaims the name of the owner: Ḥamdū Razūq. The typical unleavened bread can be seen in various stages of preparation. Balls of dough on the tray by the oven have been prepared for flattening. The baker in the background is shaping the dough into a flat bread, while the other baker is stacking freshly-baked bread on the low table in front of the shop.

At the far left can be seen a seated woman with a covering over her face.

مخبز
الصورة: ماتيليوس إيلو، عام ١٩٣١

على باب المخبز لافتةٌ كُتِبَ عليها اسم المالك: حمدو رزوق. يمكن رؤية الخبز التقليدي الخالي من الخميرة في مراحل مختلفةٍ من التحضير. حُضِّرت كرات العجين على الصينية بجانب الفرن تمهيداً لرقِّها. يقوم الخبَّاز الموجود في الخلفيَّة بتشكيل العجين على شكل رغيفٍ مسطَّحٍ، بينما يقوم الخبَّاز الآخر بتكديس الخبز الطازج على المنضدة المنخفضة أمام المخبز. في أقصى اليسار يمكن رؤية امرأة جالسةٌ مع غطاءٍ على وجهها.

People at a shop in the old town

Photo: Mathilius Elo, 1931

Presumably the man wearing the fez and the long robe (*Jalābiyah*) on the right is the owner of this shop.

The hardship caused by the First World War and the impact of the changes to politics and economy brought about by Western colonial rule led to dramatic changes in women's roles, especially, with greater access to the public sphere than ever before. One result of these social changes was that during the Mandatory Period gender increasingly played a central role in political and social battles over conflicting views of a future Syrian society. One such conflict was over the matter of veils. Gender segregation and development of new public spaces restricted to males were new battlegrounds for an increasingly vocal feminism throughout the Middle East in the 1930s. Many feminists argued that unveiling was the key to women's access to public space and civil discourse, while Islamic populists rejected unveiling and any public role for women. Eventually, paternalistic elements among the secular elite joined the Islamic populists in condemning unveiling. Towards the end of the Mandatory period, a petition by a group of women from Hama that called for the government to support unveiling was rejected.

Of course, neither of the women in this photo is veiled. Veiling does not seem to have been such an issue among urban lower classes and rural folk, among whom segregation of the genders was neither possible nor practicable.

مجموعةٌ من النَّاس أمام متجرٍ

الصورة: ماتيليوس إيلو، عام ١٩٣١

يُفترضُ أنَّ الرَّجل الذي يرتدي الطربوش والثوب الطويل (الجلابيَّة) على اليمين هو صاحب هذا المتجر في السوق.

أدتْ المصاعب التي سبَّبتها الحرب العالميَّة الأولى وتأثير التَّغييرات السياسية والاقتصادية التي أحدثها الحكم الاستعماري الغربي إلى تغييراتٍ جذريةٍ في دور المرأة، خاصة، مع زيادة الوصول إلى المجال العام أكثر من أي وقت مضى. كانت إحدى نتائج هذه التغييرات الاجتماعيَّة أنَّه خلال فترة الانتداب، لَعِبَ النوع الاجتماعي « الجندر» دوراً مركزياً بشكلٍ متزايدٍ في المعارك السياسيَّة والاجتماعيَّة بسبب تضارب وجهات النظر حول مستقبل المجتمع السوري. شكل الفصل بين الجنسين وتطوير أماكن عامةٍ جديدةٍ مقتصرةٍ فقط على الجنس الذكوري ساحات معارك جديدةٍ للأصوات النسائيَّة المتزايدة في جميع أنحاء الشرق الأوسط في الثلاثينيات. جادلت العديد من النسوة مسألة النقاب واعتبرن حظر النقاب مفتاح وصول المرأة إلى الفضاء العام والخطاب المدني، في حين رفض الشعبويون الإسلاميون فكرة حظر النقاب أو اعطاء أي دور رسمي للمرأة، وانضم إليهم في نهاية المطاف عناصر النخبة العلمانية في إدانة هذا الأمر. مع اقتراب نهاية فترة الانتداب، رُفِضَت عريضةٌ قدَّمتها مجموعةٌ من نساء حماة يطالبن فيها الحكومة بدعم حظر النقاب.

بالطبع لم تكن أيٌّ من المرأتين في هذه الصورة ترتدي النقاب، لا يبدو أن هذه المسألة كانت تمثِّل قضيةً من هذا القبيل بين الطبقات الحضريَّة الدنيا وسكَّان الريف، الذين لم يكن الفصل بين الجنسين ممكناً ولا عملياً فيما بينهم.

Spring Festival celebrations

Photo: Poul Jørgen Riis, 1937

View from Khān Rustm Bāshā across Murābiṭ Street during the Spring Festival. The female spectators, with their parasols, are watching the celebrations from the roof.

Syrian society was traditionally one of strict gender segregation. One manifestation of changes in society was the appearance of the cinema, which became a battleground for gender equality in Hama and other towns in Syria during the 1930s. As a public space, cinemas were gendered male and thus held to be inappropriate space for women by conservative elements. Both the Muslim and Christian religious establishments were troubled by women's attendance at films. Most films shown in Syrian cinemas were American or European, although Egyptian movies were also available. In general, it was thought that these films presented a way of life, especially relations between men and women, that was unsuitable for Syrian women. However, women insisted on their right to see films, and when the governor authorized a matinée for Muslim women in Hama in 1934, it caused an uproar. In 1936, theatres in Hama that held women's matinées had to be defended against attack. By 1938, Islamic religious authorities convinced the governor to ban matinées for Muslim women at Hama. A delegation of women was not able to convince the government to overturn the ban, so by 1939 outright prohibition of Muslim women's attendance at films in Hama was in place.

احتفالات عيد الربيع

الصورة: بول يورغن ريس، عام ١٩٣٧

منظرٌ من خان رستم باشا عبر شارع المُرابط في عيد الربيع. النسوة يشاهدن الاحتفالات من الأسطح بمظلَّاتهن الشمسيَّة.

كان المجتمع السوري مجتمعاً تقليدياً يفصل بين الجنسين بشكلٍ صارمٍ. كان من بين مظاهر التغيير في المجتمع ظهور السينما، التي أصبحت ساحة معركةٍ من أجل المساواة بين الجنسين في حماة ومدن أخرى في سوريا خلال الثلاثينيات. كفضاءٍ عامٍ، كانت دور السينما مخصَّصةٌ للذكور، وبالتالي تمَّ اعتبارها مساحةٌ غير مناسبةٍ للنساء من قبل العناصر المحافظة. أبدت المؤسسات الدينيَّة الإسلاميَّة والمسيحيَّة على حدٍ سواء انزعاجها من حضور النساء للأفلام. معظم الأفلام المعروضة في دور السينما السورية كانت أمريكيَّة أو أوروبيَّة، رغم توفر الأفلام المصريَّة أيضاً. بشكل عام، كان يُعتقد أنَّ هذه الأفلام تُقدِّم أسلوب حياةٍ، خاصةً العلاقات بين الرجال والنساء، غير مناسبٍ للمرأة السوريَّة. ومع ذلك، أصرَّت النساء على حقهنَّ في مشاهدة الأفلام، وعندما أجاز المحافظ إقامة العروض الصباحية للمسلمات في حماة عام ١٩٣٤م، أثار ذلك ضجةً كبيرةً. بحلول عام ١٩٣٨م، أقنعت السلطات الدينيَّة الإسلاميَّة المحافظ بحظر العروض الصباحيَّة على النساء المسلمات في حماة. لم يتمكَّن وفدٌ من النساء من إقناع الحكومة بإلغاء الحظر، وبحلول عام ١٩٣٩م، كان هناك حظرٌ صريحٌ على حضور المرأة المسلمة للأفلام في حماة.

Dances at the Spring Festival celebrations
Photo: Poul Jørgen Riis, 1937

رقصاتٌ شعبيةٌ في احتفالات عيد الربيع
الصورة: بول يورغن ريس، عام ١٩٣٧

Another view of the Spring Festival celebrations from Khān Rustm Bāshā. The sword and shield dance is derived from ancient dueling practices; each participant carries a sword and protects himself with a shield.

The Spring Festival was introduced by the National Bloc in 1935 as an expression of national unity. The Festival took place over 15 days and tents were put up to accommodate visitors from the surrounding region and beyond, including Lebanon. The Festival ran annually until the outbreak of the Second World War in 1939.

مشهدٌ آخر لاحتفالات عيد الربيع من خان رستم باشا. رقصة السيف والترس، وهذه اللعبة مقتبسة من المبارزة القديمة، التي كانت تجري بين المقاتلين في الحروب، فيمتشق كل لاعبٍ سيفه، ويمسك ترسه المعدني المصفَّح تصفيحاً قوياً ليتَّقي به ضربات سيف خصمه.

كان لحزب الكتلة الوطنية الدور المؤسِّس لهذا العيد عام ١٩٣٥م فقد رؤوا فيه تعبيراً عن وحدتهم الوطنيَّة، اعتاد أهالي مدينة حماة على الاحتفال سنوياً بقدوم عيد الربيع من خلال إقامة مهرجاناتٍ كرنفاليةٍ وبعض الفعاليَّات الثقافيَّة والاقتصاديَّة التي تستمرُّ لمدة خمسة عشر يوماً. وكانت تأتي إلى حماة وفودٌ من كل محافظات سورية ومن لبنان أيضاً لتشارك في هذا العيد. توقَّف المهرجان في عام ١٩٣٩م بسبب نشوب الحرب العالمية الثانية.

Spring Festival horse racing
Photo: Hama Expedition, 1937

Spring Festival observed from Khān Rustm Bāshā. Hama was known as the best market for purebred Arabian horses in all of Syria. During the Festival, in addition to parading their Arabian horses down the streets of the town, Bedouin tribesmen held horse races and other contests; some riders holding a type of spear decorated with silver may indicate a game of tilting.

A poster for the Spring Festival of 1–3 May 1937 in the archives of the National Museum describes various activities, such as horse races, camel races, bicycle races, football matches, and trips to the mound at Hama and nearby archaeological sites. At the same time there were other cultural events (*sūq 'ukāẓ*), such as literary and scientific conferences, at one of which Harald Ingholt gave a presentation about the Danish excavations on the mound of Hama.

سباقُ الخيل في مهرجان الربيع
الصورة: البعثة الدنماركية في حماة

مشاهدة احتفال عيد الربيع من خان رستم باشا. اشتهرت حماة بأنّها أفضل سوقٍ للخيول العربيَّة الأصيلة في كلِّ سوريا. خلال المهرجان، بالإضافة إلى استعراض خيولهم العربيَّة الأصيلة في شوارع المدينة، أقام رجال القبائل البدو سباقات الخيل وعدة نشاطاتٍ أخرى. قد يشير بعض الفرسان الذين يحملون نوعاً من الرماح المزيَّنة بالفضَّة إلى لعبة المبارزة.

يحوي أرشيف البعثة الدنماركية على مُلصقٍ لمهرجان الربيع في١ - ٣ أيار ١٩٣٧م، يصف مختلف النشاطات، مثل سباق الخيل والإبل (الهجن)، سباق الدراجات، مباريات كرة القدم، والرحلات إلى تل حماة والمواقع الأثرية القريبة. في الوقت نفسه، يدعو المهرجان إلى فعاليات ثقافية أخرى كسوق عكاظ والذي يضمُّ حفلات أدبية وعلمية يحاضر فيها كبار الشعراء والعلماء في البلاد العربية، من بينها قدَّم هارالد إنغولت عرضاً تقديمياً عن الحفريات الدنماركية في تل حماة.

Expedition members watching the Spring Festival celebrations
Photo: Hama Expedition

Members of Danish Expedition observing the Spring Festival festivities from the roof of Khān Rustm Bāshā.

أعضاءُ البعثة الدنماركية يشاهدون احتفالات عيد الربيع
الصورة: البعثة الدنماركية في حماة

أعضاءٌ من الفريق الدنماركي يشاهدون احتفالات عيد الربيع من سطح خان رستم باشا.

Bedouin in Hama

Photo: Mathilius Elo, 1931

Bedouin spectators, possibly enjoying a horse race; however, Elo offers no explanation and it is not clear from the photo if this is part of a larger celebration.

احتفالاتٌ أخرى

الصورة: ماتيليوس إيلو، عام ١٩٣١

مجموعةٌ من البدو، ربما يستمتعون بسباق الخيل؛ ومع ذلك، ليس من الواضح من الصورة ما إذا كان هذا جزءً من احتفالٍ أكبر.

Camels crossing Shaykh Bridge
Photo: Ḥāmid al-Kīlānī

Looking towards the northeast at the Bayt al-Shaykh Bridge and Kīlānī Mansion. Laden camels are led on to the bridge towards the left bank of the river and the old town.

As we have seen in previous photographs, the marketplaces were often filled with Bedouin. The relationship between the Bedouin and the merchants in Hama was very close. The Bedouin were completely dependent on the merchants in town for the goods they needed that were only available in urban markets, as well as for the sale of their livestock and products.

قوافل الإبل تَعبُرُ جسر بيت الشيخ
الصورة: حامد الكيلاني

المنظرُ باتِّجاه الشمال الشرقي عند جسر بيت الشيخ وقصر الكيلاني. تُقاد الإبل المُحمَّلة على الجسر باتجاه الضفَّة اليسرى للنهر والمدينة القديمة.
كما رأينا في الصور السابقة، غالباً ما كانت الأسواق في حماة تعجُ بالبدو. كانت العلاقة بين البدو والتجَّار في حماة وطيدةٌ للغاية. كان البدو يعتمدون كلياً على التجَّار في المدينة للحصول على السلع التي يحتاجونها والتي كانت متوفرةٌ فقط في الأسواق الحضريَّة، فضلاً عن بيع مواشيهم ومنتجاتهم.

Camel on Bayt al-Shaykh Bridge
Photo: Poul Jørgen Riis

Laden camel on the Shaykh Bridge. The Kīlānī Mansion can be seen in the background.

جملٌ على جسر بيت الشيخ
الصورة: بول يورغن ريس

جملٌ مُحمَّل على جسر بيت الشيخ. يمكن رؤية قصر الكيلاني في الخلفية.

'Abī Al-Fidā' Mosque and Mausoleum
Watercolour: Charles Christensen, 1931

The Mosque seen from across the river.

جامع وضريح أبي الفداء
لوحة مائيَّة: تشارلز كريستنسن، عام ١٩٣١

الضريحُ يُنظرُ إليه من الجهة المقابلة للنهر.

'Abī Al-Fidā' Mosque and Mausoleum
Photo: Hama Expedition, 1933

Camel caravan on the outskirts of town, at the 'Abī Al-Fidā' Mosque and Mausoleum.

'Abī Al-Fidā' (1273–1331) was an Ayyubid prince and governor of Hama. He was also a famous historian and geographer. He built the Mosque and Mausoleum for himself in 1327. In 1925, the Literary Club of Hama, headed by Dr. Shīshaklī, gave Hama the name "'Abī Al-Fidā' City".

جامع وضريح أبي الفداء
الصورة: البعثة الدنماركية في حماة، عام ١٩٣٣

قافلةٌ من الجمال على أطراف المدينة عند جامع وضريح أبي الفداء.
كان أبو الفداء (١٣٣١-١٢٧٣م) أميراً أيوبياً وحاكم حماة. وكان أيضاً مؤرخاً وجغرافياً مشهوراً. بنى المسجد والضريح لنفسه عام ١٣٢٧م.
أَطلق النادي الأدبي في عام ١٩٢٥م، والذي وكان برئاسة الدكتور توفيق الشيشكلي، على مدينة حماة اسم «مدينة أبي الفداء» نسبة له.

Camels crossing a river
Photo: Mathilius Elo, 1931

Members of the team are out on an excursion.

The camel-herding Bedouin around Hama represented one of the last camel-breeding tribes in Syria that continued to follow a fully nomadic lifestyle. Their annual migratory cycle included summer pastures near Hama and winter pastures in the Syrian steppe to the east and southeast. By the 1930s, the railroad and motorized transport had begun to erode the usefulness of their product and their form of transportation. However, they adapted to these new conditions by using the automobile in herding livestock and as forms of transportation for tribal chiefs. The automobile allowed tribal leaders to interact with their urban partners more easily and many ended up moving into towns permanently, becoming members of the urban elite.

جِمالٌ تعبر نهر العاصي
الصورة: ماتيليوس إيلو، عام ١٩٣١

أعضاءُ الفريق الدنماركي خارج المدينة في رحلةٍ.
يُمثِّل البدو رعاة الإبل حول مدينة حماة واحدةً من آخر قبائل تربية الجمال في سوريا والتي استمرت في اتِّباع أسلوب حياةٍ بدوي بالكامل. شَمِلَتْ دورة هجرتهم السنويَّة المراعي الصيِّفيَة بالقرب من حماة والمراعي الشتويَّة في سهوب البادية السوريَّة إلى الشرق والجنوب الشرقي. بحلول الثلاثينيات من القرن الماضي، بدأت السكك الحديدية والنقل الآلي بتقليص فعاليَّة دورهم وفائدتهم كوسيلة نقلٍ. ومع ذلك، فقد تكيَّفوا مع هذه الظروف الجديدة من خلال استخدام السيارات في رعي الماشية وكوسيلة مواصلات لتنقل زعماء القبائل. سمحت السيارة لزعماء القبائل بالتواصل مع شركائهم في المناطق الحضريَّة بسهولةٍ أكبر، وانتهى الأمر بالعديد منهم بالانتقال إلى المدن بشكل دائمٍ، ليصبحوا أعضاء في النخبة الحضريَّة.

Sheep being herded across the Bayt al-Shaykh Bridge
Photo: Poul Jørgen Riis, 1936

Sheep being herded across the Shaykh Bridge, with the Kīlānī Mansion in the background.

The camel-herding Bedouin shared the pastures around Hama with sheep herders. The sheep herders also had close connections with merchants in town. In fact, the sheep were often owned by merchants, who employed nomadic tribes to care for them in the pastures.

الأغنامُ تعبر جسر بيت الشيخ
الصورة: بول يورغن ريس، عام ١٩٣٦

قطيعُ الأغنام يعبر جسر بيت الشيخ مع قصر الكيلاني في الخلفية.

يتقاسم البدو الذين يرعون الجمال المراعي المحيطة بحماة مع رعاة الأغنام. كان لرعاة الأغنام علاقاتٍ وثيقةٍ مع التجّار في المدينة. في الواقع، غالباً ما كانت الأغنام مملوكةٌ للتجّار الذين استخدموا قبائل البدو لرعايتها في المراعي.

Sheep and Bedouin near Hama
Photo: Hama Expedition

Nomadic encampment near Hama.

الأغنام والبدو بالقرب من حماة
الصورة: البعثة الدنماركية في حماة

خيام البدو بالقرب من مدينة حماة.

Meeting the Bedouin
Photo: Mathilius Elo, 1931

Bedouin children at an encampment northeast of Hama.

لقاءٌ مع البدو
الصورة: ماتيليوس إيلو، عام ١٩٣١

أطفالٌ من البدو في إحدى الخيام شمال شرق حماة.

Grain cleaning in the Orontes River
Photo: Mathilius Elo, 1931

Men cleaning cereal grain in the water of the river in front of the grain mill Al-Ḥajarayn, near the Bāb al-Nahir Bridge and the Muḥamadyah Waterwheel. Al-Ḥajarayn was one of 31 grain mills that existed in and around Hama at the time. Grain was washed in order to rinse off the dust and to separate ergot- or insect-infested grain, which would float on the surface of the water rather than sink to the bottom of the reed baskets, called *zanbīl*. The process of crop cleaning is called *muṣawil* in Arabic, and a family of professional grain washers in Hama have since taken the family name Muṣawil.

تصويل الحبوب في نهر العاصي
الصورة: ماتيليوس إيلو، عام ١٩٣١

رجالٌ من حماة يقومون بعمليَّة تصويل الحبوب في مياه النهر على مشارف المدينة أمام طاحون الحجرين، بالقرب من جسر باب النهر وناعورة المحمديَّة. عمليةُ تصويل الحِنطة تتمُّ بواسطة سلالٍ مصنوعةٍ من القشِّ يُطلقُ عليها في حماة مصطلح (الزنبيل). يتمُّ غسل الحبوب بالماء من أجل تنقيتها من الغبار، حيث تترسَّب قِطَع الحصى الصغيرة وتطفو بقايا القشِّ والقمح الفاسد على وجه الماء بدلاً من أن تغوص في قاع سلال القشِّ. يوجد في حماة عائلة (المُصّول) وقد أخذت اسمها من مزاولة مهنة التصويل.

Ploughing

Photo: Mathilius Elo, 1931

Farmer in the vicinity of Hama, using a donkey-ox combination for ploughing. Ploughs had been in use since the invention of agriculture 10,000 years ago, and from the Danish excavations we find evidence for the use of ploughshares made of stone since at least the 3rd millennium BCE.

حراثةُ الأرض

الصورة: ماتيليوس إيلو، عام ١٩٣١

مُزارعٌ في محيط مدينة حماة يستخدم ثوراً وحماراً معاً في جرِّ المحراث. استُخدِمت المحاريث منذ اختراع الزراعة قبل عشرة آلاف عام، وبفضل الحفريات الدنماركية وجدنا أدلَّةً على استخدام سكك المحراث المصنوعة من الحجر منذ الألفيَّة الثالثة قبل الميلاد على الأقلِّ.

Jamīl al-Bārūdī and beehive houses
Photo: Mathilius Elo, 1931;
Assyrian relief, Layard 1853, Plate 17

Jamīl al-Bārūdī, a notable in Hama and a friend of the Expedition, at a village near Hama. The use of houses in the shape of a beehive like these is thousands of years old in Syria. They are even depicted on a carved stone relief in the palace of the Assyrian king Sennacherib (705–681 BCE) in Nineveh. This ancient eco-friendly solution to living in extreme heat has thick walls of sun-dried brick that keep the interior cool. There are usually no windows, and the high dome collects the heat at the top of the structure. An aperture at the top of the dome lets smoke out; the steep walls allow any rainwater to quickly flow down the sides without damaging the mudbrick. In areas of extreme heat in Syria, temperatures inside the beehive houses usually range around 24°C.

جميلُ البارودي والبيوت المقبَّبة على شكل خليَّة النحل
الصورة: ماتيليوس إيلو، عام ١٩٣١؛
النقش، لايارد ١٨٥٣، لوحة ١٧

جميلُ البارودي، من أعيان مدينة حماة وصديق بعثة التنقيب الدنماركية، في قريةٍ قرب حماة.

استُخدم هذا الشكل من البيوت الطينيَّة على شكل خليَّة النحل منذ آلاف السنين في سوريا، حتى أنها صُوِّرت على نقشٍ آشوري في قصر الملك الآشوري سنحاريب (٦٨١-٧٠٥ قبل الميلاد) في نينوى. يُعدُّ هذا النوع من البيوت المقبَّبة حلاً قديماً وفريداً لمواجهة المناخ الصحراوي ودرجات الحرارة المرتفعة فهي أقلُّ امتصاصاً للحرارة مقارنةً مع الأسطح المستوية، وتُساعد سماكة الجدران المبنيَّة من الطوب المجفَّف بالحفاظ على البرودة في الداخل.

تُضفي القباب العالية مزيداً من الفراغ الداخلي ممَّا يدفع بالهواء الساخن للتجمُّع في الأعلى. تَسمح جدران القبَّة شديدة الانحدار لمياه الأمطار بالتدفُّق بسرعةٍ على الجانبين دون الإضرار بالطوب الطيني المجفَّف. في المناطق شديدة الحرارة في سوريا، تتراوح درجات الحرارة داخل هذا النوع من البيوت المقبَّبة عادةً حوالي ٢٤ درجةً مئويةً.

Coffee is served

Photo: Mathilius Elo, 1931

In the village of Qalʿat al-Maḍīq, northeast of Hama. The nearby archaeological site of Apamaea is famous for its mosaics. A woman wearing a traditional outfit for this region is serving coffee to a member of the Expedition. Women in rural areas appear to have been more relaxed about wearing the veil and fully covering their hair.

تقديمُ القهوة

الصورة: ماتيليوس إيلو، عام ١٩٣١

في قرية قلعة المضيق شمال شرقي حماة، بالقرب من مدينة أفاميا المعروفة بلوحاتها الفسيفسائيَّة. إمرأةٌ ترتدي زياً تقليدياً لهذه المنطقة تقدِّمُ القهوة إلى أحد أفراد البعثة الدنماركية. يبدو أنَّ المرأة الريفيَّة كانت أكثر ارتياحاً بشأن ارتداء الحجاب وتغطية شعرهن بالكامل.